Preface

UNESCO and the Bernard van Leer Foundation both see training, based on active learning methods, as one of the most important ways to build the capacities of early childhood staff and their target groups by developing skills and strengths. It can also be an effective way to disseminate the learning from projects as well as the principles on which they work.

More and more, trainers and educators are focusing their curriculum on an interactive approach, that views adults and young children as active learners experiencing hands-on exploration of many diverse items. This approach seeks to provide an optimal environment for people to learn in their own individual manner and at their own individual level of development. Content areas in instruction are naturally interrelated as they are in real life, thus leading to learning being more a process than just a collection of facts. This methodology is well illustrated in this manual.

This book is a companion volume to *Enhancing the Skills of Early Childhood Trainers: A Training Pack,* also published by UNESCO and the Bernard van Leer Foundation. It grew out of training events conducted within the Early Childhood Joint Training Initiative in Africa, initiated by the Bernard van Leer Foundation, UNICEF, UNESCO and Save The Children US. The activities described were tested over a period of three years at international level within the Joint Training Initiative training events, at country level with national early childhood trainers and with early childhood practitioners at family and programme level.

The initiative sought to give trainers an experience of what active learning should be and to create an environment in which their knowledge could be applied to concrete situations. Nineteen participants from nine African countries, all early childhood trainers, worked with four international facilitators to internalize and apply experiential, participatory learning methods and principles to the content areas of Early Childhood Development.

This manual is a record of the experiences of the participants and facilitators in developing the skills of those who are preparing and supporting parents, family members and early childhood workers to care for young children. The participants in the initiative included: from *Ethiopia*, Aregash Abreha and Simret Mamo (Ministry of Education); from *Ghana*, Mabel Afenya (Ministry of Education) and Sarah Opong (Consultant, UNICEF ECD Programmes); from *Kenya*, Esther Kariuki (District Centre for Early Childhood Education) and Israel Komora (National Centre for Early Childhood Education); from *Malawi*, Efinita Banda (Ministry of Women's and Children's Affairs and Community Services), John Bisika (Malawi Institute of Education), Chalizamudzi Mutola and Mary Padambo (Association of Pre-school Playgroups); from *Mauritius*, Coormayah Appadoo and Christiane Sip Chong (Ministry of Education); from *Namibia*, Niki Abrishamian (UNICEF Project Officer), Leah Namoloh (Children's Desk, Namibia Council of Churches), Francina Soul (Directorate of Community Development, Ministry of Regional and Local Government and Housing) and Hope Tait (Ministry of Education); from *Uganda*, Edinance Bakehena (National Curriculum Development Centre) and Yunia Obua-Otoa (Consultant); from *Zanzibar*, Zuleikha Khamis (Nkrumah Teachers' College) and Hadiya Sultan (Pemba Pre-school College); and from *Zimbabwe*, Julia Kainga and Patricia Murevesi (Ministry of Education).

The facilitators were: Kate Torkington (the then Head of Training, Bernard Van Leer Foundation), Michael Gibbons (Save the Children US), Margaret Irvine (Independent Training and Educational Centre, South Africa/Rhodes University) and Cassie Landers (UNICEF Education Cluster). Cyril Dalais (Early Childhood Development Senior Advisor, UNICEF) acted as observer.

It is hoped that the training techniques and modules presented in this manual will facilitate the implementation of early childhood training sessions and enhance the skills of trainers, parents and care-givers in this area, and that the manual will be of value as a means of preparing the ground for the longer-term process that will ensure the continued development of active, participatory, experiential learning approaches and their acceptance as an integral part of early childhood training programmes.

Early Childhood Education

Education
A Training Manual

Margaret Irvine

Early Childhood Education
A Training Manual

The Teacher's Library
Bernard van Leer Foundation | UNESCO Publishing

Published in 1999 by the Bernard van Leer
Foundation, BP 82334,
2508 EH The Hague, The Netherlands
and UNESCO, 7, place de Fontenoy,
75352 Paris 07 SP, France

ISBN 92-3-103612-2

Illustrations: Margaret Irvine

Composed by Éditions du Mouflon,
94270 Le Kremlin-Bicêtre

Printed by Imprimeries des Presses
Universitaires de France, 41100 Vendôme
© Bernard van Leer Foundation /UNESCO 1999

Contents

Foreword

Early Childhood Education: A Training Manual is a companion volume to the *Training Pack, Enhancing the Skills of Early Childhood Trainers,* also published by the Bernard van Leer Foundation and UNESCO.

Colin N. Power, Deputy Director-General for Education at UNESCO, wrote in the Foreword to the *Training Pack*: 'The aim of this *Training Pack* is . . . to promote the learning process and give trainers an experience of what active learning should be. It advocates a learner-centred approach and the creation of an environment by trainers and trainees through which new knowledge and competencies can be acquired and applied to concrete situations.'

The training manual carries these ideas several steps further. It grew organically from the Early Childhood Joint Training Initiative in Africa, initiated by the Bernard van Leer Foundation, UNICEF, UNESCO and Save the Children (USA). The Initiative sought to give trainers an experience of what active learning should be and to create an environment in which their knowledge could be applied to concrete situations.

Nineteen participants from nine African countries, all early childhood trainers, worked for three years with four international facilitators, to assimilate and apply experiential, participatory learning methods and principles to the content areas of early childhood development. The trainers then trained *in situ* national trainers in these approaches, thus establishing a loose network of early childhood trainers throughout sub-Saharan Africa, united by a commitment to experiential, participatory learning.

During the three years, the nineteen 'core' trainers and four facilitators shared the experience of two training events, the result of which is this manual. The first was held in Johannesburg, South Africa, in February 1995, and the second in Harare, Zimbabwe, in February 1996. The manual was ready for production before the third and final training event, held in The Hague, Netherlands, in May 1997. It is hoped that subsequent editions of *Early Childhood Education* will include activities from The Hague training and, more importantly, from the continuing training events of the African trainers.

The development of a training manual from the experience of training is the reverse of the conventional approach, in which a training course is planned and prepared, then tested in several pilot-testing sites, and revised accordingly. In the case of this manual, it emerged from the activities developed during the training events. The facilitators provided a broad structure for the training programme, but the outcome and learning came mainly from the interaction between all participants, including the facilitators.

Although published jointly by the Bernard van Leer Foundation and UNESCO, the manual is owned by the Joint Training Initiative participants – it is their work over three years that is recorded in it. At the end of each of the two training events, participants were provided with a rough copy of all that had occurred during the training. The manual is a merging of these two copies. The highest tribute goes to Margaret Irvine, one of the facilitators in the Initiative, who took on the task of editing the raw material. She not only succeeded admirably in this task but she is also responsible for the lively illustrations that make the manual itself come alive.

We believe that *Early Childhood Education* is now a very worthy companion publication to the *Training Pack, Enhancing the Skills of Early Childhood Trainers,* and, we trust, of real interest and use to early childhood trainers worldwide. We also believe that it will be a useful training manual for trainers of primary-school teachers. Experiential participatory methods can be applied to any content areas.

For the moment, we are glad to recommend this manual as a companion to the the training pack and as a useful tool for training early childhood trainers. It takes an approach that is practical and easy to follow, which builds on the existing skills and knowledge of trainers and encourages personal and cultural interpretations. Above all, the manual can help trainers to develop a greater confidence in themselves as people as well as in their training abilities.

KATE TORKINGTON (BERNARD VAN LEER FOUNDATION)
JOHN BENNETT (UNESCO)
October 1998

Introduction

Much attention has been given over the years to the training of adults who are directly involved with children in early childhood programmes in education, health or community development settings. The focus however has been mainly on the early childhood curriculum and relevant activities for children. The training of trainers working with adults involved in early childhood programmes, however, has either not been given attention at all, or the approach has been very formal, in that participants are required to listen to lectures from 'experts' and 'specialists', and prior experience and learning are disregarded.

The Early Childhood Joint Training Initiative has aimed specifically at enhancing existing knowledge and skills using the participatory, experiential methods that are most appropriate for adults. This manual derives from the experiences of the facilitators and participants in the Initiative in developing the skills of those who are preparing and supporting parents, family members and early childhood workers to care for young children. It is therefore an adult education manual for early childhood rather than an early childhood curriculum manual, and builds on the experiences of the participants within the Initiative. The participatory, experiential approach builds on the strengths and the experiences of the participants as a starting point for further learning. Each participant has a vast store of knowledge and skills gathered from his or her own early childhood experiences and adult life. Not only must this store be drawn upon to develop further knowledge and skills within the group, but it must also be used to synthesize universally applicable key learning points. This is done by integrating the 'internal' knowledge of the participants and their colleagues with the 'external' knowledge of other resources such as books and 'early childhood specialists'.

The manual begins by dealing with the participants' own experiences as learners and as children in order to build both a method for working with adults and a child-centred curriculum. Working with adults includes both the functions of policy-influencing and training. These are integrated within each individual at all levels, from the parent, the community worker, the early childhood worker and the teacher through to early childhood policy-makers and trainers at local and national levels. In this manual, the two functions have been separated for the sake of the manual design.

In keeping with the participatory experiential approach is the principle and practice of teamwork. This is reflected in the manual not only in the use of small learning groups for participants, but also in the partnering of the facilitators for each training event. It is important to build a strong and empathetic relationship between the trainers before embarking on the training event.

The purpose of the manual is to help to build the training capacity of those who work in the early childhood field. As it concentrates specifically on early childhood trainers, it can very easily be used in conjunction with other resources for early childhood curricula, adult education and community development.

This set of activities has been tested over a period of three years in nine African countries at both international level within the Joint Training Initiative training events, at country level with national early childhood trainers, and with early childhood practitioners at family and programme level. One of the most important outcomes of the Joint Training Initiative has been the increase of confidence and enhancement of self-image in the participants, whose prior experience and knowledge have been heard, respected and built upon to develop with them new training methods, content and approaches to policy development.

The terms 'trainer' and 'facilitator' have been used interchangeably throughout the manual.

Overall purpose and objectives

> ## THE EARLY CHILDHOOD JOINT TRAINING INITIATIVE

Purpose

To support the development of more and better early childhood services and experiences for children and families.

Objectives

- to help to build the training capacity of those who work in the early childhood field;
- to influence early childhood policy.

> ## THE TRAINING-OF-TRAINERS MANUAL

Purpose

- to help to build the training capacity of those who work in the early childhood field by building on their existing experience;
- to enable trainers to act as agents of change in their areas of operation and countries in line with the purposes of the Early Childhood Joint Training Initiative.

Objectives

- to promote the use of experiential participatory training methods congruent with the principles of social development;
- to give emphasis to the family and community context as key areas of early childhood development;
- to clarify the role of the agent of change and to develop plans of action to effect change within the areas and countries involved.

Using the manual

This manual is designed to be used either as a full training course or section by section. The activities are sequenced and each activity leads on to the next.

There are ten sections in the manual:

1. The facilitator as learner.
2. The facilitator.
3. The child.
4. The family context of early childhood development.
5. The community context of early childhood development.
6. Planning, action and reflection.
7. Influencing policy and raising awareness.
8. Making plans of action.
9. Reflections.
10. Tools for planning and evaluation.

We suggest that you first read through the whole manual to get a sense of the flow of the activities before using the session plans. Once you have a good idea of the purpose, content and method of the whole manual, adapt each session with the facilitators with whom you work so that the needs of the participants who will be attending the training event are met and cultural differences taken into account. This is a very important step in making the manual your own. Once you have tried out the sessions and the manual, you will be able to adapt it further.

We would be interested to hear how you have adapted the sessions and about the new ones you have devised as well as about the outcomes of the training you have done using the manual. The resources used in the development of the manual are listed at the end of this book. We have tried to ensure that all resources are acknowledged. If we have not listed a resource, we will correct this omission in later editions.

The programme

Each day consists of about 6½ hours of training time, excluding breaks for tea and lunch.

Programme and sessions (Estimated number of hours, depending on the group)

The facilitator as learner (7 hours)

- Welcome and introductions
- Working together
- Expectations
- How adults learn
- Reflections

The facilitator (10 hours)

- Introduction
- The training cycle
- Surveying trainers' needs
- Learning styles
- Forming a learning community
- The Four-Open-Questions method
- Reflections

The child (14 hours)

- Introduction: personal stories
- The likes of childhood

- What is childhood?
- How children learn
- Fostering healthy adult–child interaction
- The child-centred curriculum
- Play in the first year of life
- Ensuring a stimulating environment for the 3-year-old
- The value of traditional games
- Reflections

The family context of early childhood development (8 hours)

- Introduction
- Where do children learn basic skills?
- Working with parents
- For fathers only: their role in early childhood development
- Partnerships with families
- Reflections

The community context of early childhood development (8 hours)

- Introduction
- Who helps children to develop in the community?
- Community-based approaches to early childhood development
- Community participation and mobilization
- Homeless children
- Reflections

Planning, action and reflection (about 2 days)

- Introduction
- Integrating method with content
- Giving and receiving feedback
- Designing and presenting a training session
- Synthesizing our experiences in training
- Reflections: implications for practice

Influencing policy and raising awareness (10½ hours)

- Introduction: communication
- Influencing policy and raising awareness
- Convincing donors
- Influencing politicians
- Setting up task teams
- Being an agent of change
- Reflections

Making plans of action (about 12 hours)

- Introduction
- Planning the training cycle and planning to influence policy
- Planning for evaluation
- Presentation of highlights of plans
- Reflections

Reflections (8 hours)

Shared reflections
- Introduction and response to plans of action
- Review of expectations and objectives
- Evaluation and closing ceremony

Reflections on action
- The More and Better River: charting the journey
- Personal stories of change
- Final reflections

The design
of each training session

Each of the training sessions is designed for use with a small group of participants (twenty-five at the most). When the facilitating team is working with more participants than this, it is imperative to expand the team of facilitators and to work in more than one venue. Each training session follows the same pattern.

Title

This gives the name of the session.

Time

A very approximate time is given for the session as a guideline only. The timing will depend on the number of people in the group and the newness of the participatory method of training to them. It is important to keep a lively pace in the sessions but also to gauge the interest and depth of thinking in which the participants are engaged so that timing can be adjusted there and then.

Objectives

These are very clearly stated: they are the specific outcomes of each session the facilitator plans to achieve through the steps in the session. At the end of the training, the participants should be able to demonstrate the knowledge, skills and behaviour named in the objectives for the session.

Steps

The steps describe in sequence each of the tasks that the facilitator gives to the participants in order for them to produce the expected outcomes.

Watch points

These are advisory notes for the facilitator to assist him or her in running the session smoothly. They have been developed from our experiences in presenting the sessions.

Key learning points

This is a very short summary of the main points that the facilitator needs to know before presenting the session, and which need to be drawn from participants during the session either through the activities themselves or in the summary session at the end. The facilitator needs to spend some time researching these key areas in written references and through discussion with 'authorities' in the field to build up a body of 'external' knowledge about early childhood development, community development and adult education. It is important to supplement the participants' 'internal' knowledge with this 'external' knowledge where necessary. The key learning points can be given to the participants at the end of the training session as a handout or 'top up' of knowledge.

Illustrations

The drawings accompanying the sessions attempt to give some idea of the layout of the room, flip charts or typical outcomes of sessions.

Preparing for a training event

A great deal of preparatory work needs to be done by the facilitators in order to present a high-quality training event. Planning should begin some time before the event is held. The co-facilitators need to discuss and work out their own set of visions for the training event, their own values and a set of norms that they can use to model co-operation and partnership to the participants. Here are some steps to take in planning:

1. Find out through listening, observing and discussion, the specific needs for training.

2. Find out who will be attending the training event or cycle, and how many participants there are likely to be.

3. Find out about the community and work backgrounds of the potential participants.

4. Find out about the learning needs and interests of the participants (what the participants want to learn, as well as any special physical needs).

5. Make sure that each participant is fully supported by his/her organization or institution and in turn is aware of his/her responsibility and accountability to the organization.

6. Make sure that there is adequate funding for the event.

7. Set up a clear financial plan and bookkeeping system.

8. Plan the overall design for the training event, including key objectives.

9. Prepare the logistics for the training event: venue, accommodation, transport and food, and finalize times for the training event.

10. Form a training team of facilitators and develop a common set of values and a philosophy about training.

11. Find out about and contact relevant resource people and sources of technical information.

12. Ensure that all information is transmitted to all participants well in advance.

Welcome and overview

Objectives

- to give participants information on the training event and roles and responsibilities of participants and facilitators;
- to give information about logistics.

Materials needed

- name tags (one for each person);
- materials and information for each participant as necessary;
- programme for the training event written on flip chart;
- purpose and objectives of the event written on flip chart.

Methods used

- information-giving in plenary;
- discussion in plenary.

Steps

1. The facilitators prepare the training venue in advance so that it is welcoming.

2. As the participants arrive, they are greeted and given a name tag on which they write the name by which they prefer to be called.

3. Participants are introduced to each other informally by the facilitators as they register.

4. Once everyone has assembled, the facilitators formally welcome all the participants to the event.

5. The origins and purpose of the event are stated and discussed as required, and the overall plan for the event is stated and agreed upon.

6. The roles of the facilitators, the participants and the organizations of the participants are stated (according to the discussions held before the training event with each participating organization and individual) and discussed as needed.

7. Logistical information, such as tea, lunch times and venues, starting and ending times, accommodation, transport, is given.

Important points to consider

1. Setting the atmosphere is important and having a pre-prepared training venue, wherever it is, helps participants to feel welcomed by the facilitators and gives a sense of importance to the proceedings.

2. It is important to take into consideration the needs and expectations of the participants as well as the planning needs of the facilitators.

3. All participants need to have a clear understanding of the purpose and objectives of the whole programme before they arrive for the first training event so that they will be better able to implement plans of action after the event.

4. The roles and responsibilities of the facilitators are described in later chapters.

5. The roles and responsibilities of the participants include:
    *   active participation in the training programme;
    *   active participation in the implementation phase including reporting back to organizations or institutions, adapting plans according to need within the principles and guidelines of the programme, carrying out plans of action and evaluating progress;
    *   a continuing active attention to the needs and changing circumstances of the trainers, families and children with whom the participants work.

6. The training event is relevant for all who are working with adults, as well as for those who work directly with children.

Purpose

> to form a learning community
> to clarify plans and expectations of the training event
> to examine assumptions about learning and teaching

Training sessions

(TIMINGS ARE APPROXIMATE)

1. Welcome and introductions

(2 HRS)

2. Working together

(1 HR 50 MINS)

3. Expectations

(1 HR 10 MINS)

4. How adults learn

(1 HR 20 MINS)

5. Reflections

(30 MINS)

CHAPTER 1

The facilitator as learner

1. Welcome and introductions

Objectives

- to introduce participants and facilitators to each other;
- to begin to learn about and to celebrate each other's similarities and differences;
- to begin to understand the different environments in which we live and work.

Materials needed

- flip-chart paper and markers;
- a 'Bingo' grid for each person.

Methods used

- a game in plenary for the first part;
- discussion in area groups for the second part.

Steps

A. INTRODUCTIONS

1. The facilitators welcome everyone to the workshop and ask the participants to each find a partner whom he or she does not know or does not know well. Each partner then introduces himself or herself to the other, giving:
   • a preferred name to be called by;
   • area in which he or she lives;
   • one item of information about himself or herself (including any stories about travel experiences).

2. Each participant then takes a turn to introduce his or her partner to the group.

B. 'BINGO!': CELEBRATING SIMILARITIES AND DIFFERENCES

3. The facilitators give each person a 'Bingo' grid with a pencil or pen and explain the activity. Each person:
   • begins only on the given signal;
   • walks quickly around asking other participants the questions in each block of the 'Bingo' grid and ticks each time a 'yes' answer is given;
   • asks only one question per person so that they interact with as many people as possible;
   • as participants fill up their grids, so they shout 'Bingo!' and sit down.

4. Once all are seated, participants are asked for comments on the activity and for comments on similarities and differences between participants.

C. INTRODUCTION TO EARLY CHILDHOOD ENVIRONMENTS

5. The facilitators then ask participants to get together in area groups to decide quickly on one strength and one challenge in early childhood in their area. The participants take turns to share first the strengths and then the challenges. A facilitator writes each one up on to flip-chart paper for display as the participants talk.

6. The facilitators ask the group for synthesizing comments on the activity and a short discussion on early childhood strengths and challenges is encouraged.

Watch points

This activity may take a long time to complete. Allow this to happen if necessary, so that participants begin to learn about each other and to feel confident about speaking in the group.

Make sure that everyone feels included as part of the group from the beginning of the event.

born before the establishment of the United Nations	likes chilli peppers	supervises over ten people in the job	teaches at a university
lives in an area near a river	has a Master's degree	has visited this venue before	has written a book or an article
has more than three children	has visited another country	speaks three or more languages	took a day to travel here
would like to go shopping in this workshop venue	is married	has no children	uses a computer
likes to dance	works directly with children	comes from an area that grows bananas	is a vegetarian
is a Christian	not married and eligible!	is a Muslim	met another participant last night

Key learning points on developing a learning community

1. In participatory, experiential learning, the participants are the main resource for advancing the process of planning and learning.

2. People work together and learn best in a group once they know each other. They need to feel comfortable and relaxed before they can begin to trust one another, share experiences and learn together.

3. Trust can be built from understanding where people come from and how and why they think and act as they do. Some time needs to be given to this process at the beginning of a workshop.

4. Once a group identity is built, people work well together. This can be done through various activities or 'ice-breakers' that involve getting to know one another and are useful in helping people to concentrate on the task and issues at hand. The activities the facilitators plan for this process need to be non-threatening, for instance working together first in pairs before talking in the full group. This can occur through interaction with one another and by making sure that each person feels able to speak and participate freely. Even if people do know each other, they may not be ready for discussion and interaction if there is not an initial warming-up activity to help them to focus on the event.

5. If the participants do not know each other, the facilitator can devise activities that will assist everyone to be introduced to each other and to build up a group spirit. Everybody should feel comfortable with each other and with the facilitator. Activities also need to be failure-proof and not embarrassing to the participants.

6. The group per facilitating team for the participatory approach should not be larger than about twenty-five. The best discussion group size within this for constructive group processes to occur is between five and eight people, which enables everyone to speak and participate.

7. To achieve a productive group process also requires time, as the group has to 'grow'. A learning group will evolve after two or three days of intensive interaction, often after passing through a short crisis where group spirit dips. These crises are natural in participatory group processes, and often the facilitator has to allow them to take their course, while privately counselling certain participants who are affecting group progress. Such crises can be used to evolve group spirit and build teamwork if the facilitator manages them well.

8. Participatory learning events can be exhausting, because everyone is required to intervene, to think, to reflect and to make decisions.

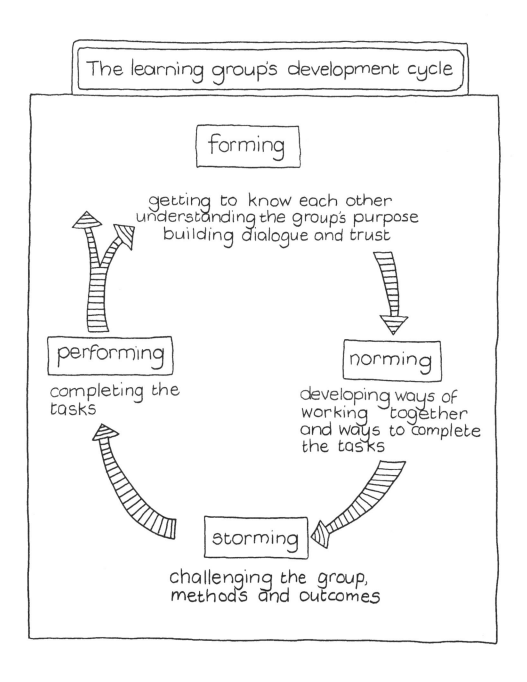

The learning group's development cycle

forming

getting to know each other
understanding the group's purpose
building dialogue and trust

performing

completing the
tasks

norming

developing ways of
working together
and ways to complete
the tasks

storming

challenging the group,
methods and outcomes

2. Working together

Objectives

- to form small learning groups;
- to identify the values that are held by participants and their communities and shape each individual's life;
- to develop a set of guidelines for working in harmony based on the values of the participants.

Materials needed

- four pieces of paper per small learning group and pens;
- wall signs **'GROUP NORMS'** and **'VALUES'**.

Methods used

- plenary and small-group discussion;
- a three-minute role play pre-prepared and acted by the facilitators. One facilitator begins:
  'My family taught me to value . . .'
  and the other facilitator responds:
  'In the community in which I live, . . . is valued' and so on.
  The facilitators try to show different values as well as similar ones.

Steps

A. FORMING LEARNING GROUPS

1. The facilitators explain that most of the work will be done in small learning groups where participants will have the greatest opportunity to participate and ask participants to walk around finding others who were born in the same month. Each of these month-groups then combines as necessary to form 'learning groups' of about four to a maximum of five people.

2. The groups then sit together for the activities which follow.

B. DEVELOPING GROUP VALUES

3. The facilitators dramatize for about three minutes a discussion about their values (see role play above).

4. In the learning groups, the participants are asked to each take a turn to describe briefly their own values and where they come from. A scribe in each group makes a note of the values as they emerge.

5. In plenary, each learning group takes a turn to give one value which is written down by one of the facilitators. There is general discussion around these values once they are all written down and a final list is made.

C. DEVELOPING GROUP NORMS

6. The learning groups re-form to discuss guidelines based on these values that will help the group to work together.
    The guidelines are written as observable behaviour. The learning group must agree on each guideline and its applicability to all customs and cultures in the larger group.

7. Each group then chooses the four most important guidelines or norms and writes each on a separate piece of paper.

8. In the plenary session, participants take turns to put one norm at a time on the wall. Each norm is put up under another if they are similar, or next to another if different (a self-categorizing activity).

9. The facilitators invite clarification and further discussion on the norms developed so far. Additions are made as necessary.

10. The group then adopts the norms for the training event and discusses ways in which the norms will be kept by the group.
    The facilitator can suggest the use of 'yellow cards' to be waved by the participants when a norm is broken. (This idea comes from the world of soccer.)

Watch points

1. The facilitators need to be aware of values and norms that may contradict each other and be ready to deal with any conflict that may arise.

2. Group norms need to reflect the underpinning values of the participants and therefore should be generated or at least adopted after discussion by each new group, rather than imposed from outside the group by the facilitators.

3. Norms can best be upheld if they are clearly understood and accepted by the group and if sanctions are agreed upon by the group as a whole make sure that this occurs.

4. Norms need to be written clearly and simply so that they reflect or indicate observable behaviour rather than attitudes only, for example, **'Wait until the person has finished speaking before speaking oneself.'**

5. The facilitators may bring the attention of the group to the norms at times during the training event to remind them of their existence or to ask whether there is a need for additions or amendments to the norms.

Key learning points on values and norms

1. Values can be described as the established ideals of life, custom and ways of acting that the members of a given society or group regard as desirable.

2. Norms are the rules that govern our lives and are accepted ways of doing things within a community. They are based on our values.

3. Norms adopted by the group help to protect the individual in the group as well as the group itself and to ensure that learning occurs in a safe environment.

Further points about values and norms

1. Values arise from the community and family as well as from experience. Each individual may have a different set of values as may each community and nation. For example, in the African experience, <u>Ubuntu</u> embraces the values of humanness, empathy, humility, mutual respect, compassion, dignity, mutual sharing and caring, whereas in the European or American experience, the values of individual striving, ambition and achievement may sometimes be seen as being uppermost.

2. It is important to explore the values and beliefs of different people with whom we work and particularly to explore our own values in order to understand norms and behaviour. We need to respect our own positive values but also to accord equal respect to those of other peoples.

3. Our own value system processes our ideas about people, places and things; our values will affect, for instance, the way in which we view children, their education and care.

4. Some values are common to all people, for instance:
   • fairness and justice;
   • integrity and honesty;
   • human dignity;
   • service;
   • quality or excellence.

5. Effective educationists work according to a known value system. This means that such educationists know:
   • what is important to themselves and to those who work with them;
   • what is good for the organization;
   • how to decide what is right, based on a concern for children's rights and human rights;
   • how to apply this knowledge to their day-to-day actions.

6. Norms are the ways in which we apply this knowledge to our day-to-day actions. It is important for any group of people working together to be clear about their common values and accepted norms or ways of working together. This assists them in achieving the tasks they set for themselves.

3. Expectations

Objectives

In the light of the purposes and programme for the event:
- to clarify personal expectations of the training event;
- to clarify expectations of the participants' organizations for the training event;
- to balance the needs of the participants with the plans of the facilitators.

Materials needed

Strips of paper for writing expectations (one expectation per strip), flip-chart paper and pens.

Methods used

- learning group discussion;
- plenary discussion.

Steps

A. PERSONAL EXPECTATIONS

1. Each participant discusses his or her own personal expectations of the training event in the learning groups. They are then written down on small pieces of paper by the individual participants and pinned up on the wall.

2. The plenary group reads these silently and is invited to ask for points of clarification on individual expectations.

B. GROUP EXPECTATIONS

3. Each set of participants from a particular area or organization then forms a group to discuss that area's or organization's expectations of the training event. These are then written down on the flip chart and posted on the walls.

4. Each area/organizational group then explains to everyone the expectations of their constituency of the training event and their own role in meeting these expectations.

C. BALANCING EXPECTATIONS AND OBJECTIVES

5. The facilitator asks for points of clarification from the group. Any areas of conflict or omission between expectations and objectives are noted.

   Areas of conflict and omission are noted on a flip chart and plans are made to adapt the programme, or to ensure that the issues are addressed in another forum.

   The facilitators explain that these expectations will be used to assist in reflecting on the training event at the end of the event.

Watch points

Ask each group to report back only those points that have not been covered by the other groups.

Key learning points on expectations for a training event

1. The objectives that the facilitators have for the training event need to be clearly described to the participants at the very beginning of the event.

2. The objectives are based on the stated needs of the participants as a result of the preliminary survey of needs carried out before the training event.

3. It is important to discuss expectations of the training event with the participants in the beginning to ensure that the facilitators and planners of the training event have correctly interpreted the survey of needs that they carried out before planning the event.

4. Time needs to be given for this in each workshop or meeting.

5. Any changes to the training programme can be made at this stage. Discussion on how to incorporate needs expressed by the participants that are not covered sufficiently by the objectives may have to take place.

6. The facilitators may need to continue to make adjustments to the programme as it unfolds and as participants identify needs not previously perceived by them or by the facilitators.

7. After the objectives and expectations have been discussed, the facilitator should then give an outline of the programme for the event. Any issues that arise from the objectives and expectations, and are not incorporated into the programme, should be clearly recorded on an 'issues' board and plans made to address them either during the event, if relevant or at some later stage outside of the event, and by the appropriate persons.

8. The participants' expectations are evaluated during as well as at the end of the training event to see whether needs have been met.

4. How adults learn

Objectives

- to clarify assumptions about learning and teaching;
- to make explicit the philosophy and biases of early childhood training.

Materials needed

- flip-chart paper and pens;
- philosophy of the Initiative written on flip-chart paper.

Methods used

- individual work;
- pair work;
- plenary discussion.

Steps

1. The facilitator asks participants to slowly relax, close their eyes and remember a time in life when they had an extraordinary learning experience:
   - what were you learning?
   - who was helping you to learn?
   - how did the person or persons help you to learn?
   - how did the learning take place?
   - what were the ingredients for success?

2. Each participant turns to a neighbour and discusses this experience. Under the guidance of the facilitator, participants randomly share their experiences under the headings above and a list of responses is made on the flip chart.

3. The facilitator asks the participants how these ideas can guide them in this training event and in the whole Initiative. Responses are written up on flip-chart paper.

4. The facilitator then states his or her own philosophy and biases (see key points) and asks for comments from the participants.

Key learning points about learning

1. Everyone is able to learn through experience, and practice and experience are central to learning.

2. Active, experiential learning activities are more effective than passive learning activities.

3. The best way to help people to learn is to pose questions rather than solutions: learning needs to be emphasized over teaching.

4. Every learning programme needs to be tailored to the needs of the participants.

5. The facilitator and the participants share responsibility for learning:
   - the role of the facilitator is to know the learner and his or her needs, to organize the learning environment, pose problems and questions, to facilitate action, discussion and reflection, and to ensure that the key learning points are integrated into the learning;
   - the role of the learner is to take responsibility for his or her own learning and to be committed to supporting the learning of colleagues and the group, as well as to develop and use a critical approach to learning.

6. Individuals' cultural backgrounds are significant for the way in which they learn.

Further points about learning and teaching

1. Experiential, participative approaches to learning are appropriate to all adult learners at all levels and for all those involved in early childhood (parents, caregivers, workers in health, education and community development, primary-school teachers, as well as adult-educators and teacher-educators).

2. The principles underpinning this approach are:
   - the empowerment of people and communities;
   - building on the strengths of individuals and communities;
   - the development of confidence and greater control over their own lives of people living in disadvantaged circumstances.

3. Experiential learning is based on the belief that participants should:
   - have greater control over their learning;
   - build on their own experience;
   - develop their own self-confidence and thus empower themselves.

4. The participation and involvement of learners are essential in this approach.

5. **Pedagogy** is the art/science of teaching children and is characterized by the following:
   - inferior roles (children) and superior roles (teachers);
   - the teacher is the central figure in the learning process;
   - the teacher gives and the pupils take;
   - the teacher's only responsibility is to teach and is thus resolved of any responsibility for ensuring that real learning takes place;
   - the dependent role of young children requires that the teacher should be in authority, but many recognize that the more learner-centred approach of andragogy applies also to children (e.g. the child-centred, learning by discovery approach).

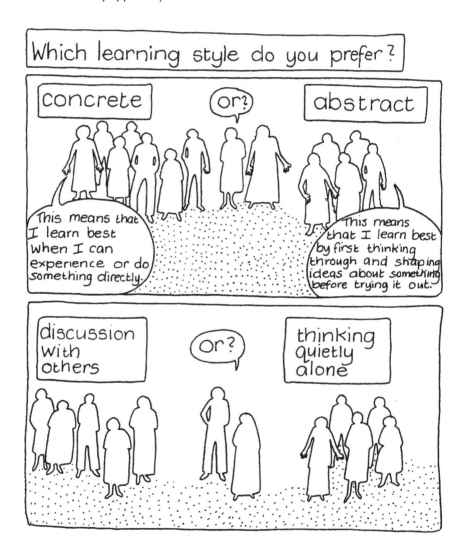

6. It has long been believed that the pedagogical approach is also suitable for adult learners. It is however, **unsuitable** because it depends on the compulsory presence of the learners, and adults, like the teacher, have a great deal of knowledge, experience from previous learning and practice. Adults have developed opinions and beliefs that prepare them for dialogue, not for acceptance of a passive, receiving role.

7. **Andragogy** is the art/science of teaching adults as adults, not as children. The underpinning beliefs in andragogy are that:
   - emphasis should be on learning rather than on teaching;
   - adult learners share responsibility with teachers for their own learning;
   - adult learners are actively involved in the learning process;
   - a teacher of adults adopts a very different role from that of pedagogue:
     - to understand the personal and social history of the individual,
     - to arrange the learning environment to promote experiential learning,
     - to create and pose problems to be resolved,
     - to facilitate dialogue and reflection on the learning experience.

5. Reflections

Objectives

- to reflect on the methods used during the day;
- to reflect on the learnings of the day.

Materials needed

Methods grid (on flip chart) and individual evaluation sheets.

Methods used

Plenary and individual work.

Steps

1. The facilitator puts the flip chart showing a range of methods that can be used for learning up on the wall and explains the terminology used. The group is asked to identify which methods they have experienced during the day, and these are marked on the grid (this grid may be used every day during review of the day).

2. Each participant then receives an evaluation sheet to fill in individually:
   'I learned . . .'
   'I enjoyed . . .'
   'I didn't like . . .'
   'I want to try to . . .'

3. The facilitator asks the participants to comment on the day and to synthesize their thoughts on the outcomes of the day.

4. The participants are asked to hand in their sheets for the facilitator to read (to be given back the following day).

5. The facilitator then asks each participant to make up a two-minute story about himself/herself to tell to the rest of the group the following day.

6. Thanks are expressed to everyone and the training event is adjourned.

Key learning points on reflection on the day's events

1. Consideration of the learnings and events of the day assists participants to reflect on what has been learned.

2. In reflecting on the day, participants are able to synthesize critically what has been of use to them.

3. If participants are able to evaluate quietly by themselves as well as in a small learning group, this assists them in evaluating critically the content and method. This is especially so when the reflection period is guided by the facilitator with open-ended questions.

4. The facilitator needs to take serious note of what is said in the evaluation, extract those issues that can be acted upon at once by the facilitator or participants and either act upon them immediately (if, for example, they concern the smooth running of the event) or ask for proposals for a plan of action from the participants. It is useful to have a time during the following session to report back on any decisions or actions taken with regard to the evaluations.

Purpose

> to reflect critically on training practice
> to identify participatory and experiential methods of training from one's own and each other's experiences

Training sessions

(TIMINGS ARE APPROXIMATE)

1. Introduction

(30 MINS)

2. The training cycle

(1 HR)

3. Surveying trainers' needs

(1 HR 30 MINS)

4. Learning styles

(30 MINS)

5. Forming a learning community

(1 HR 30 MINS)

6. The Four Open Questions method

(1 HR)

7. Reflections

(1 HR)

CHAPTER 2

The facilitator

1. Introduction

Objectives

To reincorporate the group for the work of this section.

Materials needed

Flip-chart paper and pen.

Methods used

Individual work within the plenary.

Steps

1. The participants sit in a circle. The facilitator welcomes everyone and asks them (including the facilitators), to spend a minute briefly telling the group more about themselves:
   - who I am (if there are newcomers to the group);
   - what thoughts I had during the night about what has taken place so far;
   - how I feel today.

2. Any issues that need to be followed up are written down on flip chart either for attention by the facilitators or for discussion during the following days.

3. The objectives for the section and the agenda for the day are given to the participants after comments and suggestions have been discussed.

Watch points

1. Ensure that the day starts off in a lively manner. This will help to set the tone for the day.

2. If people join the group late, it is important that all participants introduce themselves so that the group, which changes in character with the addition of new people, can re-form itself and carry on with discussions.

2. The training cycle

Objectives

To discuss the elements of the cycle of training when planning a training event.

Materials needed

- chart with a circle drawn on it entitled 'The Training Cycle';
- large labels for sticking on to the chart:
    - needs of participants, their organizations and the intentions of the participants,
    - overall goal of the training programme,
    - planning,
    - implementation of plan/training event,
    - evaluation,
    - follow-up activities.

Methods used

- silent individual work in plenary;
- plenary discussion.

Steps

1. The facilitator sets up the large chart on the wall and places the labels next to it in a random group.

2. The group is asked to place the labels on the chart in what they believe to be the 'correct' order (clockwise), starting from the top.

3. Individuals in the group take turns to do this in silence, while the group observes the pattern of the silent debate that emerges from the positioning of the labels.

4. Once the process of attaching, moving and re-moving the labels has gone on for some time, the facilitator asks individuals to explain why they prefer to put the labels in a certain order and then discusses with them the development of a training cycle.

Watch points

1. The silent debate can continue for some time; the facilitator should be careful to stop this process at a time when interest is still high, but when participants have had time to think about the process of the cycle.

2. There may be a need during the debate to duplicate labels so that the process can incorporate more steps; for example, the participants may identify the need for a needs assessment at more than one point on the cycle.

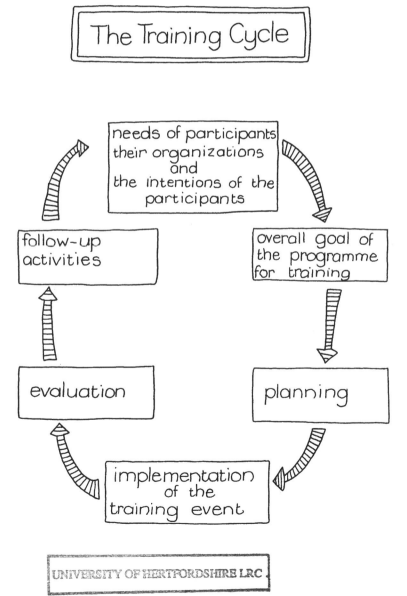

The Training Cycle

needs of participants
their organizations
and
the intentions of the
participants

overall goal of
the programme
for training

follow-up
activities

planning

evaluation

implementation
of the
training event

Key learning points on the training cycle

1. The broad steps to be followed in planning a training programme are similar for all programmes.

2. Training is a process rather than a one-off event, and a training event cannot be organized in isolation from the other activities in the cycle. A support programme needs to be put into place from the beginning of the programme.

3. The training cycle consists of various elements which interact with each other throughout the cycle – once the first process of goal setting has been completed, it needs to be revisited at a later stage during the cycle.

4. The needs of the participants on the training programme, as well as their organizations, must be taken into account for planning any programme of intervention. Not only will they inform the general planning of the programme, they will also give clear direction for the specific outcomes that must be planned for each section of the programme. This **survey of needs** will also ensure that participating individuals and organizations will commit themselves to the programme if they help to define it and believe that the outcomes are relevant to themselves and their situations.

5. The **overall goal** should be carefully worked out so that it is clear and understandable to all. It should be shared with and accepted by participants before coming to any course.

6. The **planning** for the programme can only be done once the overall goal has been set. Planning needs to reflect this goal at all times. The goal is a useful beacon or indicator to keep referring to while planning the specific objectives and the training activities for the programme.

7. Once the planning has been completed in detail, the programme is **implemented**.

8. During the training as well as at the end **evaluation** of the programme is conducted to ensure that the facilitators keep on track according to the needs of the participants.

9. The activities (content and method) of the event are evaluated in the light of the goals and specific objectives of the training event, and with regard to the applicability of the outcomes to the working environment of the participants (the participatory approach is used for evaluation).

10. **Follow-up activities** are planned and carried out once the evaluation has shown the way forward. The follow-up activities can include support visits, further needs surveys, further training events, etc.

3. Surveying trainer needs

Objectives

- to identify some general baseline information about training needs among participants;
- to practise information gathering;
- to examine group processes.

Materials needed

Prepare a brief questionnaire consisting of the four questions below, one question per page for easy collating later.

1. Whom do you train in the course of your work?

2. What do you feel are your greatest strengths as a trainer?

3. What training methods have you felt most comfortable using in the past?

4. What specific skills, ideas and methods do you hope to gain from this training event?

Methods used

- interviewing in pairs;
- collating in groups;
- discussion in plenary.

Steps

1. Introduce the survey and briefly explain that evaluation of the training event requires collection of information on training methods (baseline information) on which to base assessment of development and growth.

2. Give out the questionnaire to each pair of participants. They conduct paired interviews for about forty minutes by asking each other the questions and writing down the answers on the papers.

3. Form five learning groups. Four of the groups each take one question and collate the answers for reporting back to the plenary.

4. The fifth group observes the ways in which the other groups do this work. They report back to the full group on patterns of leadership, how conflict is managed, how the groups make decisions and on any other observations they make on how the groups work together.

5. The four groups give their reports to the plenary and the facilitator explains that this information will be used throughout the rest of the event and Initiative to help to keep the training relevant to the participants.

6. The fifth group reports on group processes and discussion is held as needed on the issues raised.

Key learning points on surveying training needs and on group processes

1. It is important at the beginning of any training event to find out exactly what the needs of the potential participants are as well as their previous experiences and expectations for the training.

2. Exploration of the extent to which expectations have been met can then be undertaken as well as an investigation into further needs.

3. The participative, experiential approach offers opportunities for participants to practise group skills. These skills include:
   - leadership;
   - conflict management;
   - participative decision-making.

4. Working in groups can be a good way of encouraging participants to work co-operatively and supportively.

5. Successful participation in a small group is based on the principle of respect for each member of the group. The way in which respect is shown is dealt with when devising group norms at the beginning of the training event.

6. Small group work encourages people to participate and to use their own experiences as part of the process of building up a body of knowledge. Participants are invited to express themselves, to share information and to co-operate in building knowledge together. Freedom of choice about whether to participate and at what level also needs to be respected, however, and no person should feel compelled to do or say anything or to take part against his or her will.

7. Patterns of leadership will hinge on the freedom of choice to participate and how to participate. Leaders will therefore encourage members of the group rather than demand, will listen empathetically, ask enabling questions and ensure that everyone has the opportunity to participate at his or her own level (i.e. the leader will ensure that group norms are upheld so that all are able to exercise their rights and their responsibilities as part of a group).

8. Conflict and decision-making are determined by the leader's and group members' abilities to listen well, to be sensitive to body language, to ask relevant questions, to focus on the task at hand and to work towards decisions that are acceptable to all members (joint problem-solving).

4. Learning styles

Objectives

To heighten awareness of differences in learning styles that will affect both learning and teaching methods.

Materials needed

Two pairs of placards depicting opposite learning styles:
- Practical (concrete) experience versus theoretical (abstract) thinking;
- Thinking quietly alone versus discussion with others.

Methods used

Individual work within plenary.

Steps

1. The facilitator introduces the activity by explaining that people seem to have a general tendency to learn a certain way, that is, a learning style, that they prefer. This session is designed to help participants to become more aware of their own preferred learning styles and to consider the implications of the styles for learning and teaching.

2. The facilitator puts concrete/abstract signs up on the walls opposite each other, indicating the imaginary line between them, and gives an example of concrete versus abstract learning styles, for example: Do you learn best by directly experiencing or doing something, or do you prefer to think through and shape ideas about something first?

3. Participants place themselves somewhere along the line or continuum between the two signs in a spot they think best describes their own learning style. They observe where others are placed, especially in relation to themselves.

4. The facilitator puts up the second set of signs 'Thinking Quietly Alone' and 'Discussion in Groups', and explains the continuum by asking, 'Do you learn best quietly thinking by yourself or talking a problem through with others?'

5. Participants place themselves somewhere along the line or continuum between the two signs in a spot that they think best describes their own learning style. They observe where others are placed especially in relation to themselves.

6. The participants are asked to comment on the needs of learners with their particular preference and these points are recorded on flip-chart paper.

7. Participants then describe in small groups what they see as the implications of these learning styles for training and their work.

8. All flip-charts are put up on the wall for reading and comments, and the information is 'banked' for the later session on guidelines for facilitation.

Watch point

This session can generate many different ideas and issues about learning and teaching which can be pursued in later sessions; ensure that points are recorded and stored for this purpose.

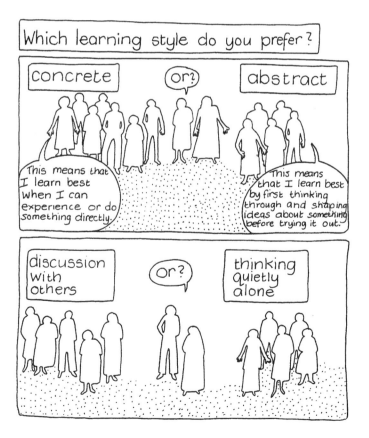

Key learning points on learning styles

1. Four different experiential learning modes that people use have been identified by various writers, including Kolb (see Book Four of the Training Pack, 'Rationale for Experiential/Participatory Methods')
   - concrete experience;
   - reflective observation;
   - abstract conceptualization;
   - active experimentation.

2. Kolb states that one learning style is not superior to another, but that we develop learning styles that suit us best as individuals. Early educational experiences shape our learning styles and we are taught how to learn through our early experiences. This has implications not only for the way in which adults learn but also for the way in which young children are taught.

3. People learn in a combination of all four of these ways depending on the learning situation, though each person does have a preferred way of learning and doing.

4. The participative and experiential training method developed by the Initiative gives particular emphasis to practical, concrete experience and discussion with others, but does not ignore the need for theoretical abstract thinking or the need to think quietly alone. The sessions and activities in the manual draw on all four learning styles.

5. When devising training events, the four learning styles need to be taken into consideration and used when planning the sequence of activities. This will add variety and texture to the planning, and cater for all participants' needs for action and reflection, concrete experience and abstraction.

5. Forming a learning community

Objectives

To reflect on how a training event is facilitated in order to form a healthy learning community.

Materials needed

Prepare a bicycle diagram, labelling one wheel 'Group Process' and one 'Task', and a set of five key-elements charts, one for each group:
- establishing a safe/respectful learning climate;
- getting to know each other;
- forming groups and establishing norms;
- reviewing the learning plan and defining expectations;
- sharing experience through practice;
- critical self-reflection.

Methods used

Role play and group discussion.

Steps

1. The facilitators stage a short role play (about two minutes) in which they argue about whether to start with the work of the event immediately or whether they should spend time forming the group first.

2. The facilitator shows the diagram of the bicycle and asks the group 'How does the bicycle help the rider to get to the destination?' (The back wheel of a bicycle is attached to the chain and **propels** the rider on the journey while the front wheel **steers** the rider towards the destination) and then explains that the **group process** (forming a learning community) in a training event can be seen as the propelling force while the **task** (the specific objectives of the training event) can be seen as the steering mechanism.

3. The facilitator then says to the group, 'We made a choice to spend a lot of time on the group process (back wheel) in order to form a learning community at the beginning so that the task of the training event would be more effectively carried out', and gives each learning group a key element for forming a learning community.

4. In the learning groups, participants are asked to discuss:
   - how the key element has been achieved up to now during this training event;
   - what other methods can be used (In your home/cultural context, what would be appropriate?).

5. The responses are written on pre-prepared charts.

6. All the flip charts are put up on the wall and read silently by the whole group. Each group then has a turn to answer any questions on its own chart and to add ideas.

7. General discussion is conducted as necessary on the points raised.

Watch point

Watch time-use in the groups, so that the pace of the session remains lively and brisk.

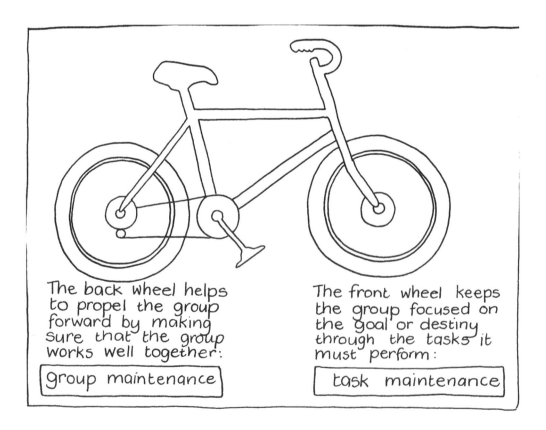

The back wheel helps to propel the group forward by making sure that the group works well together:

group maintenance

The front wheel keeps the group focused on the goal or destiny through the tasks it must perform:

task maintenance

Key learning points on forming a learning community

1. In order to build an environment based on trust and safety, and to make sure that learning can take place, the facilitators should plan activities that directly address these needs, especially at the beginning of a training event (like the propelling mechanism of the back wheel of the bicycle, it gets the participants started and travelling forward on the journey).

2. The participants, who come from different communities, need to develop a unique community in which they can learn from each other. They are strengthened by their differences as well as by their similarities. This community consists of the participants and the facilitators (all of whom are present at the training event each day).

3. When new people join the learning community (even for the day), the nature of the community changes and, to ensure that the flow of trust and learning is not compromised, the new person and the present participants should be formally introduced and become acquainted with each other.

4. The type of activity that best builds a learning community addresses participants' needs:
   - to know more about each other;
   - to understand their differences and similarities;
   - to celebrate their strengths in diversity;
   - to use their opportunities to learn from each other in a non-threatening environment.

5. These activities may not directly deal with the content of the course but should be related in some way so that the flow of the content is not broken, for instance:
   - telling each other preferred names and meanings;
   - telling stories about themselves and their environment, needs and plans.

6. Group maintenance activities can include the following actions by the facilitators:
   - calling the participants by name;
   - asking questions which seek new and relevant answers;
   - clarifying what participants are asking or saying;
   - co-ordinating or chairing the sessions and ensuring that everyone is included and that those who always talk give others a turn;
   - keeping the sense of humour in the group by making relevant jokes and allowing others to joke as well;
   - keeping the time so that tasks are completed but also so that participants do not get bored;

- varying the texture of the activities so that the pace is kept interesting (e.g. slow/fast, standing/sitting, individual/group);
- listening empathetically and actively to all inputs and ensuring that body language is relevant to the situation.

7. Task-maintenance activities that help the group to achieve outcomes and feel that the event has been worthwhile include the following actions by the facilitators:
   - initiating the discussions and posing problems rather than solutions;
   - focusing the group on the task at hand;
   - clarifying the task whenever necessary;
   - deciding on the way ahead with regard to tasks and timing;
   - taking notes;
   - closing the sessions with synthesizing activities;
   - keeping the pace at a level which is comfortable for the group.

6. The Four Open Questions method

Objectives

To observe and practise posing a problem for learning, using a code and critically analysing the problem in order to derive possible solutions.

Materials needed

- prepare a picture based on the needs of the trainers (from the survey of training needs) that illustrates problems dealing with leading a training session (e.g. participants looking bored and the facilitator lecturing for a long time);
- prepare the chart showing a problem-analysis method;
- flip-chart paper and pens.

Methods used

- brainstorming;
- fishbowl;
- group discussion.

Steps

1. The facilitator introduces the session by showing the participants a stone or twig or some other easily available object and asking them to state as many uses as they can imagine for it as quickly as possible.

2. The facilitator then names this activity 'brainstorming' and asks participants to analyse what happens when brainstorming takes place. Participants are asked to sum up with a definition of brainstorming.

3. Participants are asked to think of ways in which they tackle problems posed by participants in their own training. Responses are written up on flip charts.

4. The facilitator then links this information to the problem-solving grid and explains how it works (see Key Points) using brainstorming to elicit as many responses to each of the four questions as possible.

5. A picture describing a problem (a 'code') is put up on the wall for everyone to see and four or five volunteers are asked to form a group in front while all the other participants are asked to observe the process of using the grid and brainstorming to analyse the problem.

6. The facilitator asks the small group in turn the following questions and responses are written up by a scribe on flip-chart paper on the wall:
   • What do you see happening here?
   • Why do you think it is happening?
   • What effects do you think it may have in your situation?
   • What can we do about it?

7. At the end of the fourth question, the participants choose what they consider to be the most relevant solution to begin with and a plan of action is made step by step.

8. All the participants are then asked to discuss in small groups what they observed about the method (the fishbowl group form a separate group):
   • Was the problem effectively portrayed? Why? Or why not?
   • How did the questions assist the participants to discuss the problem? How not?
   • What other methods could be used to portray this problem?
   • In what other situations could the Four Open Questions be used?

9. The facilitator asks each group to give one response at a time to the questions until all responses are given for a question (nominal round technique), always starting with the fishbowl group.

10. The full group is asked to synthesize the key learning points on this method for facilitating responses to problems and is asked to save the ideas for the later sessions.

Watch points

Make sure that the picture is fairly simple so that the discussion is not drawn out. It is important that this session is seen as a demonstration of a method.

Key learning points on the Four Open Questions

1. Paulo Freire proposed that the most suitable approach for adult learners is the 'problem-posing' approach, which enables people to make their own decisions about solving problems and addressing challenges. (The opposite approach to this is the 'banking' approach, where the teacher remains in control of knowledge and 'gives' it to the learners as solutions to problems.)

2. The Four Open Questions are worded in such a way as to ensure that all answers are relevant and that an environment of safety and respect for each individual is generated and maintained; for example:

- the words '**you** see' and '**you** think' invite each participant to state freely their own responses rather than the 'right' responses and therefore encourage people to participate in the analysis;
- respect for each person is built into the word '**you**'. Each person's contribution is sought as a worthwhile offering to the process;
- the use of the word '**we**' when looking for solutions invites all the individuals who have been responding so far to combine strengths and understandings as a group to tackle the problem;
- the process of analysing the problem starts with the use of the senses ('**see**') and the 'real' world;
- the process of looking for cause and effect starts with the use of the mind ('**think**') and the world of theory;
- the process of looking for solutions is bedded again in the 'real' world with the use of the word '**do**'.

3. Once these four questions have elicited many, wide-ranging responses (ensuring that everyone involved has been given and has taken the opportunity to brainstorm), the possible solutions are prioritized and steps are planned in some detail to carry out the plan of action.

4. Brainstorming is a technique used to gather as many ideas as possible before deciding which ideas to focus on. People need to feel free enough to be able to voice all sorts of ideas, even those that may sound irrelevant or 'silly'. It is these ideas that help group members to think widely about a situation or problem. Comments and discussion are allowed only after the brainstorming session is over, when each point is then accepted or discarded.

7. Reflections

Objectives

To discuss critically the challenges for working in this way in one's own area and environment and its feasibility.

Materials needed

Flip-chart paper prepared for each group, headed in the first column: 'Constraints or challenges to using these participatory, experiential methods in your own environment' and a second column for responses.

Methods used

Group work and plenary.

Steps

1. The participants regroup into area or organizational groups. Each group discusses the question above and writes clearly and simply the constraints and challenges in the first column on the flip-chart paper.

2. These are then given to another area/organizational group for discussion, analysis (using the Four Open Questions model) and finally 'collegial advice' given in writing in the second column, with consultation with the first group as necessary.

3. All recommendations are written up in the first column. Each area group then displays the charts for silent reading in plenary.

4. Synthesizing comments on the outcomes and on the activity itself are given by members of the group as necessary.

5. The facilitator explains that this activity leads to the session on planning and on forming sub-regional/collegial support networks in the section on planning.

Key learning points on reflecting on action

1. Reflections can be carried out by asking participants to evaluate the usefulness of the learning outcomes in their own work and life.

2. By encouraging constraints and challenges to be analysed as well as positive experiences, participants are allowed to express their doubts in a supportive atmosphere.

3. By using the Four Open Questions to investigate difficulties, participants are able to analyse problem areas critically in a participative manner.

Constraints or challenges to using the participative experiential method in my environment	Some ideas for solving the problem

Purpose:

> to look critically at our underlying assumptions about
  * how children develop
  * children's needs
  * implications for adults' helping behaviour

Training sessions

(TIMINGS ARE APPROXIMATE)

1. Introduction: personal stories

(2 HRS)

2. The likes of childhood

(1 HR 15 MINS)

3. What is childhood?

(1 HR 30 MINS)

4. How children learn

(1 HR)

5. Fostering healthy adult–child interaction

(1 HR 30 MINS)

6. The child-centred curriculum

(3 HRS)

7. Play in the first year of life

(1 HR)

8. Ensuring a stimulating environment for the 3-year-old

(1 HR 30 MINS)

9. The value of games

(1 HR)

10. Reflections

(30 MINS)

CHAPTER 3

The child

1. Introduction: personal stories

Objectives

- to explore aspects of positive listening behaviour;
- to share aspects of personal history and experiences as children as the basis of our learning in a creative, culturally appropriate way.

Preparation needed

- the participants should be informed the day before to prepare a short story of about three to four minutes about their background or personal history as a child to tell to the group;
- participants may use any materials or objects to illustrate the story.

Methods used

- individual preparation and plenary discussion;
- individual story-telling.

Steps

1. The facilitator welcomes everyone to the day's activities and introduces the activity, stating the purpose of the session, and the timing for the stories, and asking everyone to listen carefully and supportively to each other's stories.

2. The participants are asked to think quietly for a minute about behaviour and actions they have experienced that have assisted them to talk freely and safely. The facilitator asks for points from participants at random and a list of these is written up on flip chart.

3. Facilitators may model or illustrate the story-telling process by starting with their own stories or may ask for a volunteer to begin.

4. As each story is told, the facilitator asks for further volunteers until everyone who wishes to participate has had a turn.

5. At the end of the activity, the facilitator asks for comments on the process and then on the content of the stories, where appropriate.

Watch points

1. This session is best done once a reasonably safe environment has been established because the stories can be quite emotional and intense.

2. Be prepared to help the group to listen supportively.

3. Encourage more confident or outgoing participants to tell their stories first and allow participants to share at their own speed and in their own time; these will differ according to the needs of each group.

4. Breaks should be taken together by the group where appropriate, since this activity may take a long time to complete.

Key learning points on building trust

1. People help to build trust in the group through an understanding and then acceptance of each other's diverse background and history, thereby allowing for open and frank discussion between all participants.

2. By helping participants to explore and share their own history prior to exploring the theme of early childhood development, the activity reinforces the experiential participatory nature of the training.

3. Active listening using non-verbal behaviour appropriate to the customs of the participants is an important means of building trust.

4. Listening is an art and a skill. It requires self-control and discipline to listen quietly and at the same time to observe what another person is saying through their spoken and non-verbal language.

5. We can listen in several different ways:
   - we can give the impression of listening, but not be listening at all (we often do this with young children);
   - we can listen selectively and choose what we wish to hear (we also often listen in this way with young children);
   - we may listen attentively to the words, but hear from our own point of view rather than from the point of view of the speaker;
   - we may listen empathetically, hearing all the words spoken and 'reading' the body language from the point of view of the speaker. Empathetic listening means that we seek to understand what the speaker is saying from his or her own point of view.

6. The skill of listening requires the use of the ears and the eyes. We need to show interest in what the speaker is saying through our own appropriate body language. We need to concentrate on what is being communicated.

7. We also need to guard against behaviour that 'interrupts' the speaker: for example, arguing, interrupting, passing judgement too quickly or in advance, giving unsolicited advice jumping to conclusions and letting the speaker's emotions react too directly on our own.

8. Good listening behaviour is defined by the cultural backgrounds of the listener and speaker. This may vary a great deal; for instance, it may be considered polite to listen with eyes downcast and little expression, or on the other hand, to listen by looking straight into the eyes of the speaker and being very responsive in facial expression and gesture. We need also, therefore, to 'listen' to the cultural background of the speaker.

2. The likes of childhood

Objectives

Working from the memories of the participants of their own childhood:
- to explore the needs of children;
- to draw out the knowledge about child development that participants have gained from their own experience;
- to supplement their personal knowledge with 'external' knowledge.

Materials needed

- pens and paper for each participant;
- flip-chart paper and pens.

Methods used

Individual, pair work, plenary discussion.

Steps

1. Participants each write down three things that they remember with pleasure from their own childhood.

2. In pairs, participants discuss these.

3. In the plenary circle, they volunteer some of the things they have discussed together. Partners report on behalf of each other.

4. The 'likes' are written on slips of paper that are posted randomly on the wall by each pair.

5. They are then grouped on the wall chart, with the assistance of the participants, in a way that demonstrates the needs of children, i.e. social, emotional, physical, cognitive, moral, spiritual. If any of these dimensions have not been illustrated in the 'likes', the facilitator can ask for other 'likes' that illustrate this dimension.

6. The facilitator helps the group to explore – where appropriate – the traditional ways of rearing children and helps the group to synthesize the learnings from this session.

Watch points

1. It is possible to ask for the negative aspects of the participants' childhood, but this can lead to personal distress and greater support is therefore necessary from the facilitator and the group as a whole. It is necessary to have achieved a high level of group trust to work on these negative points.

2. Participants could be asked to 'think of three things', which avoids either emphasizing negative or positive aspects, but the warm feelings that dealing with pleasurable memories invokes may be lost.

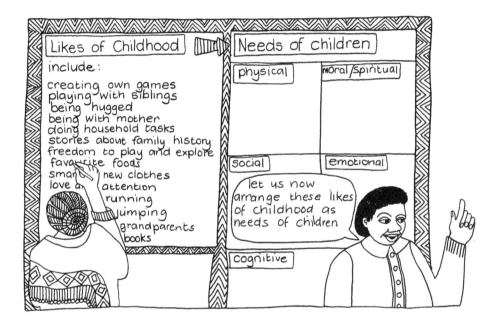

Key learning points on the likes of childhood

1. All adults have had intimate experience of early childhood development, having experienced childhood themselves and, in most instances, being parents and grandparents, aunts and uncles.

2. In line with the participative experiential method, this 'internal' knowledge and experience need to be drawn upon before 'external' knowledge is superimposed or dictated.

3. The 'established' early childhood curriculum has been categorized under the headings of physical, social, emotional, cognitive, spiritual and moral development, developed from the needs of the child, but the connection to these roots is often lost through the use of jargon or the technical language of the discipline.

4. People relate to the reality of child development through their own authentic experience. Through focused discussion with others based on this experience, they can access relevant 'established' early childhood theory.

3. What is childhood?

Objective

To explore the beliefs and values attached to childhood in different cultures.

Materials needed

Flip-chart paper and pens for groups to record their own discussions.

Methods used

Small groups and plenary discussions.

Steps

1. In small groups made up of people from different geographical areas, the participants discuss the following questions and compare their individual experiences within the group:
   - How is 'childhood' defined in your own area or culture? (and what ages does it encompass?)
   - How do you define 'early childhood'?
   - What values and beliefs does your culture or area hold about childhood?
   - What do you think that children have as the goals of childhood, and does this contrast with what adults aim for in their upbringing of their children in your area or culture?

2. In plenary, the facilitator asks each group to report back on one question at a time.

3. Once all the answers concerning one question are received, the facilitator helps the group to explore the similarities and differences in their beliefs and values about childhood. All questions are dealt with in this way.

4. A brief synthesis of the learnings of the activity is developed through summary statements made by volunteers among the participants.

Watch points

1. There are no correct answers to these questions and there are considerable variations within areas and cultures. The facilitator may have to assist participants to show empathy and understanding towards each other's backgrounds, values and beliefs, while debating the merit of the different beliefs.

2. These are very difficult questions that societies have been grappling with for centuries; the groups may experience some frustration in not being able to arrive at definitive or clear answers.

3. This activity may leave the group feeling unclear and vague, and needs to be followed by a more practical activity that results in very clear outcomes.

Key learning points on childhood

1. Each society may define childhood in different ways and according to different time-frames. Early childhood is often defined as the years between birth and 5 or 6 or 7 years of age, or between birth and 9 years of age.

2. Each family within a community may have different beliefs and values about childhood stemming from that family's own specific experiences, background and history. Examples include one family's belief that a child should eat only at formal family meal times and another family's belief that the child should eat when hungry.

3. Communities themselves will have differing sets of values and beliefs based on their own histories and environments. For example, one community may believe that children should be seen and not heard while another community may value children's questions and chatter as a focal point in the family.

4. These sets of values and beliefs need to be explored and debated in a respectful way before a curriculum is devised for the young children in the families making up the wider community.

5. Respect for the beliefs and values of people needs to be shown in actions and behaviour most appropriate to the community. This behaviour should be defined by and for early childhood personnel with members of the community they serve (when beliefs need to be challenged, this should be done in a courteous and empathetic manner).

6. If beliefs need to be challenged, for example on the grounds that they are known to be harmful to children, then it is always a good idea to discuss first a cultural belief that is clearly positive before gently challenging the less positive belief. This can best be done by listening carefully and empathetically to the discussion around the belief.

4. How children learn

Objectives

- to explore ways in which children learn;
- to describe participants in the learning process, and their involvement and role.

Materials needed

Photographs and pictures of children playing and working within their peer groups, families and communities (enough for the whole group to make choices).

Methods used

Small group and plenary discussion.

Steps

1. The facilitator asks the participants to form themselves into their learning groups and representatives of each group to come and choose one picture from the pile in the centre of the room.

2. Each group discusses the following questions around the two pictures:
   - **How** are the children learning?
   - **Who** is involved in the learning (what is each person's role)?

   Each group in turn then shows the picture to the full group and responds to the two questions above.

3. The facilitator invites participants to discuss and debate the responses as necessary and then to summarize the learnings from the activity.

Watch points

This is a good introductory activity for a discussion on the early childhood curriculum. It should be fairly lively and quick.

Key learning points on how children learn

1. Children learn best:
   - when they are ready and wanting to learn a specific skill or information;
   - when they learn through 'doing' – active participation and practice of their new skills for example by dramatizing or role-playing, handling materials and equipment, experimenting, listening to a story;
   - through observation of a child or adult and then imitation of that process or behaviour;
   - when they are able to use their senses to explore the environment – seeing, feeling, hearing, smelling and tasting.

2. Young children learn through play. Play facilitates development. This is because the 'as if' nature of play allows children to perform actions that are more developmentally advanced than those they can actually achieve.

3. Play fosters a sense of self-esteem and competence, supporting and reinforcing the child's capacity for effective action.

4. Play helps children to grow, learn and explore. It builds children's curiosity, language, social skills and understanding of adult roles. Play also helps children to master their newly emerging perceptual and motor skills.

5. The role of the adult or older child in helping the young child to learn includes:
   - providing a supportive environment such as encouraging the child, allowing the child to try out new skills, demonstrating new skills, listening carefully to the child, giving required information;
   - being available for the child to call upon when necessary for assistance or advice and to participate when required in the games and activities of the child;
   - ensuring that the child has plenty of time to play.

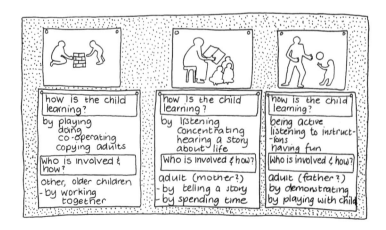

5. Fostering healthy adult–child interaction[1]

Objectives

To identify specific helpful and harmful behaviour of adults in support of child development.

Materials needed

Flip-chart paper and felt tip pens for each group.

Methods used

- small group and plenary discussion;
- role play (drama).

Steps

1. The facilitator introduces the session and links it to the previous activities as another step in the process of defining the early childhood curriculum in learner-centred terms.

2. In their learning groups, the participants discuss the following questions:
   - About half of the learning groups discuss **in what ways adults discourage the healthy development of children (through harmful behaviour and attitudes).**
   - The rest of the groups discuss **in what ways adults can best foster a child's development (helping behaviour and attitudes).**

3. The groups then devise short (two minutes at most) dramas showing these types of behaviour and present them to the plenary.

4. The participants debrief these roles as they wish to in order to explain what they were portraying and how they felt while acting out the roles.

---

1. Adapted from a training session designed and presented by the participants from Zanzibar.

5. The lists of behaviours are reviewed and participants discuss these particularly with regard to cultural differences.

6. Synthesizing comments are made about the outcomes of the activity.

Watch points

1. The participants need to present specific behaviours and actions such as 'give encouragement **by smiling** at the child'.

2. There will be cultural differences in the ways in which helpful and harmful behaviours are seen. Ensure that these are discussed as needed in the groups.

3. Encourage role-plays to be short and to the point, and allow participants to debrief after they have finished acting.

Key learning points on fostering healthy adult-child interaction

Adults best promote the child's development through the following helpful behaviour and actions:

- communicating feelings of love and support through appropriate body contact, closeness and gestures;
- communicating appropriate levels of trust and respect for the child as a fellow human being (e.g. respecting children's feelings);

- providing clear, simple and consistent rules that are relevant to the child's developmental stage;
- maintaining appropriate body and eye contact with the child according to cultural norms;
- responding to the child's behaviour through appropriate sounds and words, for instance, encouraging, praising, responding where relevant, focusing on and naming objects, processes and feelings that the child is busy with;
- following the initiatives of the child within the constraints of the health and safety of the child;
- expressing happiness at being with the child through facial expression and gesture, and showing confidence in the child's abilities to succeed;
- sharing feelings and insights into processes and objects;
- providing a secure and safe environment for the child.

6. The child-centred curriculum

Objectives

To develop a shared set of preliminary statements on the concept of a child-centred curriculum.

Materials needed

- flip-chart paper and pens;
- three stickers each for voting or some other method of marking preferences.

Methods used

- individual work, small group and plenary discussion;
- voting procedure.

Steps

1. The facilitator introduces the task, which is a culmination of all the activities preceding this one.

2. Individuals first make a list of what they think should be included in a child-centred curriculum.

3. In the learning groups, the participants discuss and debate the group members' lists and make up a list of ten statements that reflect agreed elements.

4. The statements are written up on separate pieces of paper and posted on the wall by the groups in a way that categorizes them as similar (underneath one another) or different (alongside one another).

5. All participants walk round reading the statements and points of clarification are called for as necessary.

6. Each participant then votes for the three statements he or she considers to be most important by pasting the stickers next to the three preferred statements.

7. The participants then count the votes and the ten most popular statements are listed as those generated by the group as a whole.

8. The participants then re-form into groups according to organization or geographical area:
   - to discuss the present curriculum in their centres or organizations in the light of this definition of the child-centred curriculum;
   - to discuss steps to be taken to make the early childhood curriculum more child-centred if necessary.

9. Each group then shares a brief statement with the plenary on each of these questions and the information is recorded for the later session on planning for the future.

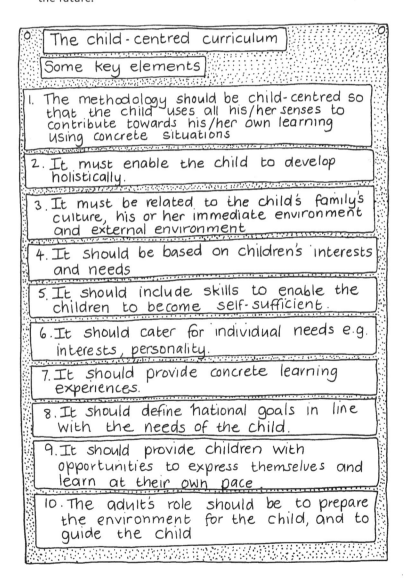

The child-centred curriculum

Some key elements

1. The methodology should be child-centred so that the child uses all his/her senses to contribute towards his/her own learning using concrete situations

2. It must enable the child to develop holistically.

3. It must be related to the child's family's culture, his or her immediate environment and external environment

4. It should be based on children's interests and needs

5. It should include skills to enable the children to become self-sufficient.

6. It should cater for individual needs e.g. interests, personality.

7. It should provide concrete learning experiences.

8. It should define national goals in line with the needs of the child.

9. It should provide children with opportunities to express themselves and learn at their own pace.

10. The adult's role should be to prepare the environment for the child, and to guide the child

Key learning points on the child-centred curriculum

1. The concept of 'curriculum' is quite broad with many different adjectives attached to it: child-centred, negotiated, socially constructed, hidden, integrated, etc.

2. Curriculum means the entire range of developmental experiences, planned and unplanned, that learners become engaged in through their participation in educational programmes.

3. Curriculum may be defined as being made up of the following:
    *   aims and objectives;
    *   content;
    *   'teaching' methods and learning methods;
    *   evaluation procedures for assessing participant progress as well as the curriculum itself in the context of the environment of the child, family and community.

4. The concept of the child-centred curriculum is based on the belief that the child's developmental needs within the family and community, and the way in which children learn should inform the method of 'teaching' and the content of any early childhood development programme.

5. The child-centred approach promotes the freedom of the child to grow and mature according to his or her own developmental needs within the needs of his or her community and the wider society.

7. Play in the first year of life[1]

Objectives

- to identify ways in which babies learn through play in the first year of life;
- to identify ways in which mothers and fathers, and early childhood workers can best listen and talk to each other about child development.

Preparation

The organizers of the training event could ask local mothers and fathers to attend this session with their babies. The reason for the session should be made very clear to them, as should the context, and they should be given the invitation well in advance so that they can prepare for the day.

Materials needed

- play items for babies, such as balls, shakers, soft toys and whatever relevant objects are used by parents of children of this age group in the area;
- pictures of mothers with babies between 3 and 12 months of age (especially if mothers and babies are not available);
- flip-chart paper and pens.

Methods used

- observation;
- pair or small group work;
- discussion in the plenary group.

Steps

1. The facilitator welcomes the parents with the babies to the session, asks the participants and the parents to introduce themselves, and states the objectives of the session.

---

1. Adapted from a training session designed by a group of the participants in the second phase of the training Initiative.

2. The participants group themselves with the parents and children (two to four in a group if possible), choose toys for the children to play with and observe how the babies react to the toys and how adults support them.

3. Each group (including both participants and parents) discusses what they have observed and then considers the following questions:
   - What do babies learn to do during these months?
   - How do the adults assist the babies to learn?

4. Each group chooses pictures of adults playing with babies to discuss as a supplement to the observation.

5. The groups discuss these issues in plenary, each giving one response to the full group until all groups have had a turn and all points have been raised.

6. The facilitator asks for a synthesis of the learnings from all of the participants on play.

7. The facilitator then asks the participants how they found the experience of working together as early childhood workers and parents with children. Comments are synthesized and guidelines for listening to each other are devised.

Watch points

1. The participants may be unused to working in a formal training environment with mothers and children. If this is the case, it may be useful to debrief the session with them after the parents and children have left the training event.

2. The importance of giving mothers opportunities to contribute in the groups needs to be stressed.

Key learning points on play in the first year of life

1. Babies like to be active and to move whenever they get the chance.

2. Babies play by using all their senses and through playing they discover their environment.

3. Everything that a baby does and the routines they are given by the adults are times for play, for instance bathing and being dressed. All activities that stimulate their bodies and their senses to develop thinking and intelligence constitute play.

4. Some of the activities that babies like are listening to sounds and songs, enjoying being touched, looking at faces, noticing their own hands, playing with fingers and toes, kicking, reaching for objects, grasping objects, releasing them, banging and playing with toys, putting toys in the mouth, playing peeping games.

5. Babies learn through interaction with an adult. It is important for the adult to be sensitive to the baby's personality and mood. All babies are different.

6. Adults help babies to learn by holding them, touching them, speaking, singing to them, repeating words, giving them objects to hold and feel, playing games like peep and catch, and helping them to move and use their senses. Adults are babies' best 'playthings' to begin with, supplemented as they grow older and more mobile, with objects.

Key learning points on listening skills

1. Facilitators need to be sensitive to the possible lack of confidence on the part of parents and in particular mothers to discuss child-rearing issues in any forum with other groups of people.

2. Good listening skills will be required to assist the mothers to discuss openly and confidently.

3. Guidelines for facilitators to follow in order to help people to talk freely and frankly, and to talk about matters that are important to them, would include the following:
   • showing an interest in what is being said and being alert;
   • noticing non-verbal signs that the speaker may give and responding to these;
   • understanding the speaker and viewing statements from the speaker's point of view;
   • being open-minded and non-judgemental;
   • mirroring the speaker's mood;
   • continuing to listen even though you think you have heard it all before;
   • being patient and respectful;
   • cultivating the ability to be silent when silence is needed.

8. Ensuring a stimulating environment for the 3-year-old child[1]

Objectives

To examine activities in the home which will be stimulating for the 3-year-old child.

Materials needed

- a variety of materials and equipment found in the home and environment;
- paper and pens.

Methods used

- group discussion;
- practical work.

Steps

1. The facilitator asks the participants to talk to a partner about aspects or areas of play in and around the home which children like being involved in. Each pair states one aspect, which is then written down on flip-chart paper, until all aspects or areas are recorded, as follows:
   - the natural world;
   - building activities;
   - the make-believe world;
   - music;
   - art;
   - sorting and counting;
   - in the kitchen;
   - in the bathroom;
   - in the garden.

2. In learning groups of four or five, participants choose one of the spheres/areas in which to make a list of activities. Lists are posted on the wall for later reading.

---

1. Adapted from a training session designed by the participants from Mauritius.

3. The groups then look for and collect household materials and equipment, and set up an activity for 3-year-olds that is both stimulating and safe for children.

4. Each group takes turns to try out the activities and to read the accompanying lists of other activities in that sphere or area.

5. The facilitator asks the participants to comment on the displayed activities and to answer the following questions:
   - Why do you think the children would like the activity?
   - What will the children learn by playing with it?
   - What is the adult's role?

6. The participants then synthesize the key learnings from this session.

Watch points

Ensure that there is enough as well as a variety of material to devise play activities.

Key learning points on providing a stimulating environment

1. Children will develop their potential for creative thinking if space, materials and time are provided. Adults should help children when required, but allow them to grow and learn independently.

2. Adults need to ensure that the environment and materials are secure and safe for children to play in and with.

3. Children do not need expensive, bought toys. A variety of simple toys and everyday materials and the freedom to experiment with them in a safe and supportive environment, are more important.

4. Materials should be accessible to children so that they can play with them when they wish. All dangerous materials should always be kept safely out of reach.

5. Children can practise large and small motor skills, learn practical skills (like copying the father or mother washing dishes, sweeping, gardening, preparing food, etc.), as well as talking and counting, etc., while playing in and around the home.

9. The value of games[1]

Objectives

To enhance participants' awareness of the importance of games for children's learning.

Materials needed

Flip-chart paper, pens.

Methods used

- individual work, small groups and plenary;
- discussion.

Steps

1. The facilitator introduces the session and asks each participant to contemplate how they played as children of between 3 and 6 years of age (what games, toys and occupations they enjoyed being involved in).

2. In small groups (randomly chosen or according to geographical area) each participant describes a particular game he or she played as a child.
   The names of the games, the instructions and materials needed to play the game are recorded on paper (one game per page).
   Materials are named and categorized as 'natural', 'scrap' or 'bought'.
   The small groups then discuss and write down the value and benefits of the games to the child's development.

3. Each group then demonstrates one game to the rest of the group.

4. Each group posts its flip-chart papers on the wall for everyone to read.

5. The facilitator asks for summary points on the games, materials and benefits.

---

1. Adapted from a training session designed by the participants from Ghana.

Key learning points on the value of games

1. Children between the ages of 4 and 6 especially like:
   * to play games that involve other children in a group;
   * role-playing (make-believe);
   * games with rules that they often make up themselves;
   * running, active games;
   * building games.

2. Games assist children to learn new skills, knowledge and behaviours including the following:
   * social skills (such as co-operating with others and learning to take turns, to win and to lose);
   * cognitive (intellectual) skills (such as thinking, speaking, counting, concentrating and memorizing);
   * physical skills (such as catching, throwing, aiming, balancing, rhythm and co-ordination);
   * moral behaviour (such as honesty and fairness);
   as well as providing great enjoyment and fun.

3. Children very often play games using natural or scrap materials which they make into new objects through imagination or creativity.

4. Some games require special materials, objects bought from a shop or especially made by an adult such as tops and marbles.

5. Many traditional children's games teach skills and knowledge needed by children in their everyday lives as well as passing on the heritage and stories of the community.

10. Reflections

Objective

To reflect on the learnings of the section 'The Child'.

Materials needed

Paper for each participant.

Methods used

Individual work and plenary discussion.

Steps

1. The facilitator introduces the session by referring to the programme listing the sessions on 'The Child' and asks the participants to think about their key learnings over this part of the training event.

2. Each participant takes a turn to describe his or her key learnings to the group.

3. The session is then closed.

Watch points

Ensure that this session is well timed so that a fast pace is maintained.

Purpose

> to review critically and redefine the family context of early childhood development

Training sessions

1. Introduction and warm-up   (TIMINGS ARE APPROXIMATE)

                                                          (1 HR)
2. Where do children learn basic skills?

                                                       (30 MINS)
3. Working with parents

                                                    (3 HRS 30 MINS)
    *   why it is important to work with parents in early
        childhood programmes   (1 HR)
    *   complementary skills and knowledge of parents and
        early childhood workers   (30 MINS)
    *   different ways of working with parents   (45 MINS)
    *   difficulties in working with parents   (30 MINS)
    *   exploring ways of developing parent education
        programmes   (45 MINS)
4. For fathers only: fathers' role in early childhood
    development

                                                    (1 HR 30 MINS)
5. Partnerships with families

                                                       (3 HRS)
6. Reflections

                                                       (30 MINS)

CHAPTER 4

The family context of early childhood development

1. Introduction

Objective

To reincorporate the group for the day's work and to reinforce the importance of 'self' in childhood and of the child within the family.

Preparation

The day before, the facilitator asks a small group of participants to prepare a short song or activity relevant to the theme of the family context of early childhood development.

Methods used

Individual contributions within plenary.

Steps

1. The volunteer participants welcome everyone and introduce a song/activity.

2. The facilitator then talks about the importance of the names given to us when we are babies because we are special and unique within our families and communities, and asks participants to tell the group what their preferred first name means, who gave the name to them and why.

3. The facilitator completes the activity by asking the participants why this might be an important activity for adults and children.

4. The agenda for the section on the family context and for the day is outlined as follows by the facilitator:
   - The theme of this component is the family context of early childhood development.
   - Infants begin their journey through life in the immediate family environment where they develop and grow as toddlers and young children. This is the principal domain of early childhood development – the family context.
   - The purpose of this set of learning sessions is to review critically our understanding of the family context of early childhood development.

Key learning points

INVOLVEMENT OF PARTICIPANTS IN THE PLANNING AND PRESENTATION OF SESSIONS

1. Once participants know each other and the facilitators, and feel comfortable with the routine of the training event, it is useful to begin the process of working with them as co-facilitators.

2. Involvement in preparation and presentation of sessions by the participants can be initiated at first by inviting them to prepare a relevant warming-up song or activity at the beginning of a session.

3. Later on, participants will wish to and be able to present sessions themselves to the group. This should be encouraged. A supportive atmosphere should first be developed where participants understand how sessions are planned, presented and reflected upon.

4. Facilitators in a training event need to model the way in which planning, facilitating and reviewing of sessions is done by them. This can best be done by inviting participants to be involved in the whole process of planning and review. In other words, these activities are carried out in the open where participants are invited to be present.

THE IMPORTANCE OF OUR NAMES

1. The Declaration of the Rights of the Child states that every child has the right to a name.

2. Ceremonies for naming children differ from community to community. The ways in which names are chosen for children differ. These are important for each person, whether adult or child.

3. Names very often have a meaning. It is important to know the meaning of one's name.

4. Naming and recognition of the name enhance self-esteem and provide a link to family and community history.

2. Where do children learn basic skills?

Objective

To initiate reflection on and interest in the family and community context of early childhood development.

Materials needed

A copy for each participant of the 'Where do children learn basic skills?' grid.

Methods used

Individual, pair and plenary work.

Steps

1. Once the participants are settled in and focused, quickly pass out the 'Where do children learn basic skills?' grid to each participant. Explain how to fill in the grid and ask each participant to work on it alone for five minutes.

2. Ask the participants to turn to an immediate neighbour and share their findings briefly in pairs.

3. In plenary, the facilitator asks, 'What are your reflections on the exercise? Where do children learn things? Only in school?'

4. The facilitator encourages some discussion on this topic and then states the purpose and steps to be taken in the set of sessions on the 'Family Context of Early Childhood Development'.

Watch points

This is an introductory 'warming-up' activity which is best carried out quickly and informally.

Key learning points

1. Children learn the majority of their early skills and attitudes from home.

2. These learnings are supplemented very often by institutions within the community: for example, religious institutions, early childhood development programmes.

3. The early childhood development facilitator needs to be aware of the importance of the home in the development of the young child and to plan programmes around this point.

Where do children learn basic skills?

Here is a list of some of the skills and attitudes that young children learn. Tick the column where you think they are most often learnt.

Add your own ideas of skills and attitudes that children learn.

	Skills and attitudes	Home	Play group or pre-school	School	Other
1	writing her or his name				
2	getting dressed and undressed				
3	washing him- or herself				
4	going to the toilet unaided				
5	eating unaided in the custom of the community				
6	knowing the alphabet				
7	sharing toys				

	Skills and attitudes	Home	Play group or pre-school	School	Other
8	putting things away				
9	respect for other children				
10	respect for authority				
11	controlling feelings				
12	understanding the religion of the family				
13	looking at books				
14	listening to stories				
15	telling the time				
16	customs of the community				
17	counting				
18	knowledge about the world				

Source: adapted from Us and the Kids pack

3. Working with parents

Objectives

- to explore why it is important to work with parents in early childhood development programmes;
- to identify the complementary skills and knowledge of parents and early childhood workers;
- to share different ways of working with parents;
- to identify some of the difficulties of working with parents;
- to explore ways of developing parent education programmes.

Materials needed

- handouts for each small group with nine statements about working with parents;
- envelopes for each small group with cut-up sets of all nine statements on separate pieces of paper;
- charts for each of the tasks and feedback.

Methods used

- small groups and plenary discussion;
- ranking activity.

Steps

1. To explore why it is important to work with parents in early childhood programmes (ranking activity):
   - briefly review the title, purpose and outline of the session;
   - give out and briefly review the attached handouts on the nine statements asking for points of clarification;
   - hand the envelopes to each learning group and state the task: in each group, discuss the statements on working with parents and then rank the statements in the order of importance perceived by the group using the following pattern:

     1st
     2nd 2nd
     3rd 3rd 3rd
     4th 4th
     5th;

- groups share their findings in the plenary, building a common sense of the many reasons why working with parents is important.

2. To identify the complementary skills and knowledge of parents and early childhood workers:
   - in the plenary group help the participants build two lists, side by side, on the flip chart; on one side a list of what parents know about a child; on the other what teachers know about a child;
   - ask the participants for a synthesis of the learnings from this activity and write this down on the flip chart.

3. To discuss different ways of working with parents:
   - once again in plenary, help the participants brainstorm a list of ways to work with parents drawn from their own experience; list these on a chart;
   - lead a discussion on implications of this list for practice.

4. To identify some of the difficulties and challenges of working with parents:
   - in learning groups, discuss and explore some of the challenges and concerns about working with parents;
   - post the reports on the wall and review them as a large group;
   - as a final step, ask participants to share one thing that caught their attention when reading the lists and to explain why it caught their attention;
   - the facilitator then highlights the key learning points with the help of the participants.

Key learning points on working with parents

1. Parents are the primary educators of young children. They know a very great deal about their own children and this knowledge needs to be respected and drawn upon by the early childhood worker in a partnership with the family.

2. Early childhood workers develop another body of knowledge about the child in the context of the early childhood programme, which in turn should be shared respectfully with the parents of the child in this same partnership.

3. There are many ways in which early childhoood workers can partner parents, for instance visiting the child and family at home, informal discussions with parents at the early childhood programme and early childhood worker/parent support groups.

4. A gap or divergence often arises between the home and the early childhood programme (the family and the early childhood worker) as a result of many perceptions and misperceptions on either side. The early childhood worker may think or believe that parents lack education or knowledge. The parents may see the early childhood worker as having expert and privileged knowledge about children which they are unwilling to share.

5. The term 'partnership' is defined as a relationship or alliance between colleagues working together for a common cause. The colleagues may have different knowledge, skills and competences that they channel to the benefit of the child and they thus need to respect each other as complementary forces. Parents and early childhood workers therefore need to form partnerships to best meet the needs of the children.

Why work with parents? Statements

HELP FOR WORKING MOTHERS

Early childhood programmes can ensure that children are well looked after while their parents work. These programmes can only be really effective if ways are found to keep in touch with parents.

CHILD-CARE SKILLS

Some parents lack the basic skills of child care. Inviting parents to spend time in early childhood development centres gives them a chance to learn from staff and other parents.

KNOWLEDGE OF CHILDREN

Parents have the most knowledge and understanding of their own children. If parents are encouraged to share this knowledge, workers can make use of this to provide better education and care for children.

SELF-ESTEEM

Some parents lack self-esteem. By spending time with parents and encouraging the development of personal skills, workers can give parents a sense of self-worth and a feeling of confidence in their own abilities to look after children.

COMPLEMENTARY SKILLS AND KNOWLEDGE

Parents have gained skills and knowledge about child development through experience. They know their own children very well. Professional workers in early childhood development have more theoretical knowledge about children in general. The best early childhood programmes will recognize this and use these two resources in a complementary way.

PARTNERSHIP

Early childhood provision is a community facility that should be responsive to the needs of those who use it. Parents should be involved in decisions to provide early childhood facilities, in discussions on how these should be managed and in the evaluation of facilities.

MUTUAL SUPPORT

People often get the best support from those who have similar experiences and similar problems. Early childhood development programmes should include opportunities for parents to meet so they can share feelings, values, attitudes and knowledge, and support each other through difficulties.

EXTRA PAIR OF HANDS

There are several tasks associated with the care of children that do not require particular training or exercise: preparing snacks, making toys, washing cups. Parents should be encouraged to do such tasks so that trained workers can provide skilled education and care.

IMPROVING UNDERSTANDING

Some parents lack an understanding of children's needs for stimulation. Parents should be encouraged to participate with workers in planning and carrying out play activities with children. This will help them understand the value of play.

4. For fathers only: father's role in early childhood development[1]

Objective

To identify effective ways to encourage fathers to be more involved in early childhood development.

Materials needed

- Group 1:   paper and crayons;
- Group 2:   case study written on paper;
- Group 3:   case study written on paper;
- Group 4:   written instructions for a drama to act out;
- Group 5:   board game (see instructions for making and playing);
- flip-chart paper and pens.

Methods used

- group work of different kinds;
- plenary discussion.

Steps

1. The facilitator introduces the topic and asks the participants to state briefly how they see fathers behaving towards their young children. Responses are written quickly on flip-chart paper.

2. Groups synthesize these comments into a statement of their experience of the opportunities and challenges facing them.

3. Participants form five groups and the facilitator gives each group an activity to do (see following group activities).

4. Each group is asked to report back on the findings of their group, except for Group 4, which presents the drama to the group and the questions for discussion after all the other reports back have been made.

---

1. Adapted from a training session designed by the participants from Namibia.

5. All the presentations are recorded by the groups and, after all presentations have been made, a general discussion is opened and a synthesis of the learnings is made.

Watch points

1. This activity is especially designed for groups of fathers, but can be adapted for use with trainers.

2. Be aware of participants' cultural beliefs and customs and ensure that this sensitive subject is handled in a way that will lead to honest and supportive discussion.

3. Positive perceptions about behaviour can be used to discuss and possibly change negative perceptions about fathers' behaviour.

Key learning points on the role of fathers in early childhood development

1. The father is a very important figure in the life of the baby and young child, and there is a need for strong ties to be developed between them from an early age, together with the mother who is usually the central figure in the baby's early months.

2. Some interactions that do take place between fathers and young children include (in Africa for instance) the following:
   • fathers and other male relatives assist in socializing male children;
   • grandfathers and older males transmit values and social mores;
   • men teach young children relevant life skills such as the identification of cattle patterns, plants, landmarks, weather, etc.;
   • fathers and male relatives collect and relate folk tales, proverbs, family history, kinship and extended community relationships;
   • men help to construct buildings and equipment, and help to produce learning materials.

3. Perceptions and beliefs about the role of the man and the father in the family and society can often prevent him taking a full and natural role in the upbringing of his young children: he may not only believe that young children are not his primary responsibility, but be supported in this belief by the women and mothers themselves.

4. Since babies and toddlers are seen as 'belonging to' their mothers and other women, fathers are perceived as distant figures even when living in the same home. Their task is to punish wrong-doing.

5. Some strategies that would recognize and reinforce the traditional role of the father while at the same time identifying and encouraging new mutually acceptable behaviour include:
   - enabling both men and women to be self-confident and assertive as individuals and as groups;
   - assisting in the formation of support groups;
   - appealing to men's self-concept as an integral part of the family unit;
   - actively involving parents and grandparents of both sexes in learning, teaching and ensuring that both sexes take on positions of responsibility;
   - encouraging men who are caring fathers and participants in family life to act as role models;
   - emphasizing equality, co-operation and respect in the curriculum.

   (Source: Bernard van Leer Newsletter, No. 65, January 1992)

GROUP 1 A POSTER

What is the most important message you as a father can give to another father?

Make a poster to illustrate the message in a way most likely to attract fathers.

GROUP 2 WOMEN'S WORK!

If tomorrow all the women in your community disappeared, how would you, as a man, run your household and look after the children? What would you do? Make a list of the activities you would need to do from the morning to the evening.

GROUP 3 PROBLEM-SOLVING

If you were a pregnant woman, what do you think your needs would be? Make a list of the things you would need to do to ensure a healthy pregnancy and baby.

GROUP 4 A DRAMA: 'THE PREGNANT MOTHER'

The group prepares to act out the following script for the participants:

'A pregnant mother is working non-stop, fetching water, cooking, taking care of the other small children, cleaning. The father is sitting chatting with some other men, reading and drinking (at one point he takes a nap). When he needs anything, he asks the pregnant mother. She brings everything to him, and continues with her work. As soon as she wants to rest, someone calls and demands something from her. The father calls for his dinner. The woman looks extremely tired.'

Questions to ask the participants are:

- What do you see happening here?
- Why do you think it is happening?
- What are the effects when this happens in your environment?
- What can we do about it?

GROUP 5 A BOARD GAME 'FOR FATHERS ONLY'

Make a board with twenty blocks marked 1 to 20

block 1 is also marked 'Start' and block 20 is marked 'Finish'

each block can be decorated with a picture of fathers and children

Make twenty cards with a question about child-rearing practice on each, for example:

- If you had a choice of giving any of the three following foods to your child, which would you choose and why? Chips, eggs, fizzy drink, meat, sweets, bread, milk, porridge.
- Name one thing you can do to protect your child from disease.
- What is the most important thing to give your child if he or she has diarrhoea?
- At what age do you think that children start to learn and to use their brains?
- Can you think of another way other than beating to discipline your child?
- What do you think children gain from playing?
- In what ways can you assist your pregnant wife?
- As a father, what are some ways in which you can support your child's growth and development?

Rules for playing the game

Each person takes a turn to roll the dice and pick up a card.

If the answer is correct according to the members of the group, you can move forward according to the number on the dice.

If, according to the group, your answer is wrong, you remain where you are.

The first person to reach the 'finish block' wins.

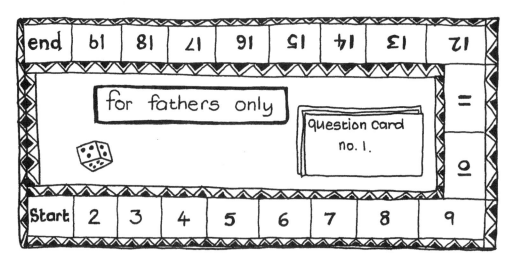

5. Partnerships with families

Objective

To develop guidelines for working successfully in partnership with parents and families in early childhood development.

Materials needed

Case studies written out for each of three groups.

Methods used

- role plays (dramas);
- plenary discussion;
- small group discussion.

Steps

1. INTRODUCTION

The facilitator states the name and purpose of the session and indicates how in order to succeed successful early childhood development work requires partnership at several levels, for example:
- between the early childhood worker and parents;
- between the early childhood worker and the community;
- between the trainer/supervisor, co-trainers and early childhood workers;
- between the early childhood trainer and policy-makers/donors.

In this session the partnership with families, especially parents, is emphasized.

2. TASK: DEVISING A GROUP ROLE PLAY

- the facilitator organizes three small groups and distributes one case study to each group;
- each group creates and performs a short role play that demonstrates the problem depicted in the case study;
- they are performed without comment between each role play.

3. PLENARY DISCUSSION

The facilitator leads the plenary in a discussion of the three role plays together following the format below:
- what happened in each role play?
- what were the problems depicted?
- what solutions do we propose?

4. TASK: SMALL-GROUP DISCUSSION

Groups are asked to replan their role plays using the lessons learnt from the plenary to transform the role plays into success stories. These are presented but not discussed.

5. CODE OF CONDUCT (SYNTHESIS)

- In plenary, the group shares any summary insights from the 'successful partnership' role plays.
- The facilitator asks for several participants to volunteer to synthesize the 'solution' ideas from all these role plays into a draft set of guidelines after the session ends.
- These guidelines are then shared with the participants the next morning for review and adoption.

Watch points

Encourage participants to make the role plays fairly short and to the point.

Key learning points on guidelines for working with families

1. Guidelines for early childhood workers when working with families might form the basis of a self-appraisal instrument and may include the following points:

   (a) Getting to know the families of the children you work with through:
   - informal visits to build friendly acquaintances;
   - informal chats;
   - sharing daily chores and experiences (drawing water, babysitting, etc.).

   (b) Identifying and getting to know family needs through:
   - observation;
   - listening;
   - chatting and mixing with everyone.

   (c) Involving parents when discussing early childhood issues by:
   - encouraging them to take part in identifying and solving problems and implementing ideas;
   - giving opportunities to families to initiate ideas.

(d) Developing a good knowledge base about early childhood development and the child-rearing beliefs and customs in the community.

(e) Knowing the country's policies relevant to family life and the rights of families.

(f) Identifying other role players in the community to pull together resources and creating a collegial relationship with other partners – developing constant contacts and maintaining them.

(g) Keeping families informed about early childhood matters, through:
- disseminating information formally and informally;
- holding meetings.

2. Guidelines for a 'code of conduct' for early childhood workers may be developed including the following points:
- respecting family values, culture, norms, beliefs, traditions and customs;
- being empathetic towards the needs of the families;
- showing courtesy and humility;
- being patient;
- avoiding demeaning the family;
- establishing trust;
- recognizing the family's knowledge and building on it;
- making parents feel valued;
- using effective communication skills and establishing ways of exchanging information;
- understanding that the early childhood workers' knowledge and skills are different but should complement those of the family.

CASE STUDY 1. PARTNERSHIPS WITH FAMILIES

'Oh, what a bother! These remote villages are so dusty in the dry season, and this house I am visiting is so dirty.

'I will probably have to eat some of that food. I can't avoid it. And I bet the mother has not even done her early childhood development activity/homework.'

This is what our friend Lota was thinking as she walked into the village to do her weekly early childhood development home visit. She then proceeded to knock at the door, greet the mother, enter and conduct her session. The mother was of course gracious, but a bit overwhelmed, tired and not at her best.

Task

First, depict the **wrong** way to make a home visit and what can go wrong as a result.

After discussion, you will have an opportunity to portray the best way to conduct this type of meeting.

CASE STUDY 2. PARTNERSHIPS WITH FAMILIES

Emanual never was very good at school. As a result, he is bound and determined as a father to ensure that his son receives a good, academic 'head start' in pre-school. He agrees to go to the parents' evening at the school to check on the academic standards for his parents' group.

During the course of the visit, Emanual gets increasingly concerned that the school seems to encourage play but not academic work.

The teacher, on the other hand, feels that the visit is going well. Her speech went well and the parents are well behaved.

Suddenly, Emanual confronts the teacher and begins demanding to know why the teacher is not teaching the alphabet and numbers in the pre-school. He obviously knows nothing about early childhood development.

Task

Depict the **wrong** way for parents and teachers to interact at a parent–teacher's meeting.

After discussion, you will have an opportunity to portray the best way to conduct this type of meeting.

CASE STUDY 3. PARTNERSHIPS WITH FAMILIES

Mamatua, a community worker, was running late. Her bus broke down on the way to the market town, delaying the two-mile walk to the village.

When she arrives she is hot, tired and thirsty. The mothers, meanwhile, are getting very tired of waiting. Their children are beginning to get hungry and uncomfortable.

When Mamatua arrives, she curtly sits and begins her lecture. As the talk proceeds the mothers get increasingly uneasy and Mamatua becomes increasingly frustrated. She finally leaves in a huff.

Task

Depict this scene in the **wrong** way for a parents group meeting to occur.

After discussion, you will have an opportunity to portray the best way to conduct this type of meeting.

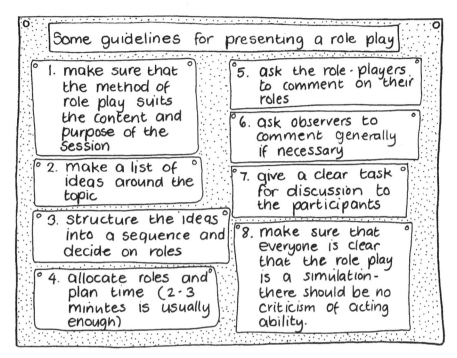

6. Reflections

Objectives

To reflect critically on the learnings of the sessions on the family context of early childhood development.

Materials needed

Paper and pens.

Methods used

- individual work, small groups and plenary discussions;
- voting procedure using stickers.

Steps

1. The facilitator invites participants to think quietly about:
   - the content of the sessions in this section;
   - the process devised by the facilitators to achieve the objectives.

2. In small groups participants air the thoughts they have had on these topics and make a list of these for reporting to the plenary.

3. The groups take turns to give one point at a time in plenary first on the content of the sessions and then on the process used to achieve the objectives. All points are written down by the facilitators.

4. Participants discuss points that need clarification or debate.

5. Each participant then receives four stickers to mark those two points in each session that he or she feels are the most important.

6. These votes identify the priority points on content and on process. Final synthesizing comments are made by participants and facilitators as necessary on the voting outcomes.

Watch points

This session needs to be lively and short so that the day ends on an active and dynamic note.

Purpose

> To review critically and redefine the community context of early childhood development

Training sessions

CHAPTER 5

The community context of early childhood development

1. Introduction

Objective

To reincorporate the group for the day's work and to introduce the section on the community context of early childhood development.

Preparation

The day before, the facilitator asks a small group of participants to prepare a short song or activity relevant to the theme of the community context of early childhood development.

Method used

Individual contributions within plenary.

Steps

1. The volunteer participants welcome everyone and introduce a song/activity.

2. The agenda for the section on the family context and for the day is outlined as follows by the facilitator:
    *   The theme of this component is the community context of early childhood development.
    *   Infants begin their journey through life in the immediate family environment and, as they develop and grow as toddlers and young children, they make their first forays out into the wider world within the neighbourhood and community setting. The community context is the second domain of early childhood development, after the principal domain of the family.
    *   The purpose of this set of learning sessions is to review critically our understanding of the community context of early childhood development.

2. Who helps children to develop in the community?

Objective

To help participants to look critically at the complementary roles of community members who support child development.

Materials needed

- charts for about eight groups in anticipation of the number of community helpers who will be identified, with spaces marked for information on the roles, capacities/resources and limitations/needs of each community helper;
- a poster of the concentric circles surrounding the child placed in the front of the room;
- small cut-outs of parents, teachers, siblings, extended family members, caregivers, etc., ready to stick on to the poster.

Methods used

- plenary discussion;
- diagrams and pictures;
- small groups.

Steps

1. In the plenary group the facilitator asks 'Who helps children develop in the community?'

2. The participants brainstorm ideas such as:
   - brothers/sisters (older siblings, cousins, neighbours' children);
   - parents, extended family adults;
   - neighbours;
   - key cultural caregivers;
   - community and clinic health workers;
   - professional caregivers and teachers.

3. As these categories are identified, the cards representing these figures are posted on the child-centred circle picture.

4. Each group then chooses a different category and discusses the following questions:
   - What can this group of people contribute to the development of the young child?
   - What resources and limitations do they have?

5. Groups discuss these questions, list these items and post their findings on the chart for everyone to read.

6. The facilitator conducts a plenary summary discussion about the composite picture of all those who help children develop, cultural differences in the roles in different countries and ways to build partnerships among these roles.

Watch points

1. There need to be two facilitators available to find and stick the cut-out figures on to the circle diagram so that the brainstorming session is not held up by the facilitators looking for the relevant pictures.

2. The facilitators should be ready to draw or write down the names of other helpers in the community as they are identified by the participants during the session.

Key learning points: 'Who helps children to develop in the community?'

1. The family is seldom isolated in the rearing of its children. Families form part of the communities in which they live through their interaction with other families in the neighbourhood and with institutions and services in the community, for instance shops, religious institutions and schools.

2. Many of the people and institutions identified in this activity can be mobilized in some way or other for the cause of optimum child development.

3. Each person and institution has particular skills or knowledge of use in early childhood development. These skills and knowledge as well as the capacity of each person to be involved, will differ from person to person and institution to institution.

4. The early childhood worker needs to be sensitive to the potential in each person and institution as well as to the limitations and needs of each.

5. The early childhood worker can build partnerships with the institutions and people in the community by making sure that he or she has detailed knowledge of the community and its networks.

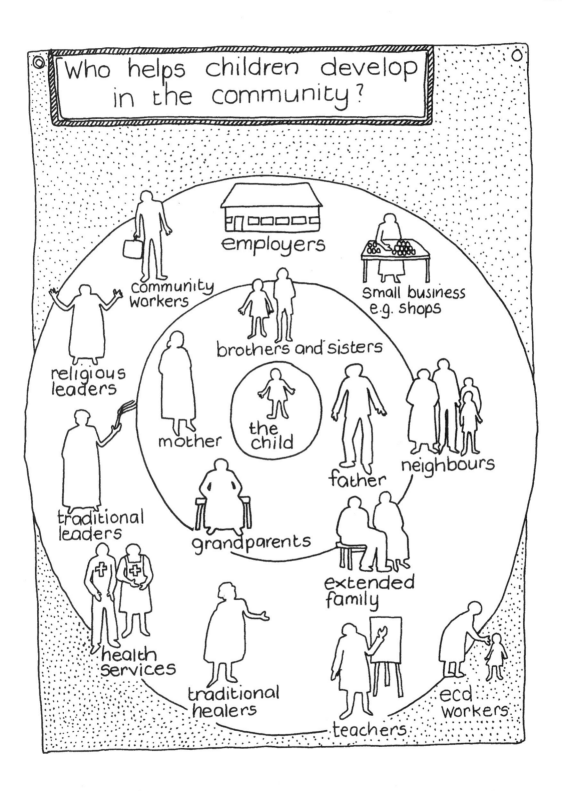

Who helps children develop in the community?

employers

community workers

small business e.g. shops

brothers and sisters

religious leaders

mother

the child

father

neighbours

traditional leaders

grandparents

extended family

health services

traditional healers

teachers

ecd workers

3. Community-based approaches to early childhood development

Objective

To review key community-based programme approaches to early childhood development in the community context.

Materials needed

Flip-chart paper and pens.

Methods used

Plenary discussion.

Steps

1. Referring to the child-in-the-circle map, explain the purpose of the session.

2. Participants individually think about one community-based early childhood development approach they have used or seen in their work.

3. Participants report at random, without repeating each other, to generate a list quickly in plenary, mentioning for instance:
   - child-to-child programmes;
   - parent education programmes;
   - home-visiting programmes;
   - community motivator programmes;
   - community early childhood development – primary school links;
   - church-related programmes such as 'Sunday school'.

4. Participants are invited to ask for information about any one of the programmes written up on the flip-chart.

Watch point

Make this session short and fast-paced to contrast with the previous session.

Key learning points on community-based approaches to early childhood development

1. Many alternatives to the centre-based model of early childhood development are being practised all over the world. They may offer a close relationship between the family and the early childhood worker, and encourage parents to attach greater value to their own parenting skills.

2. All alternatives need to be explored with the families in a community during discussions on their own specific child development needs.

3. Specifically tailored programmes can then be devised with these needs and hopes in mind.

4. Community participation and mobilization[1]

Objective

To develop shared definitions and understandings of the concepts of:
- community;
- community project;
- community participation and involvement;
- community mobilization.

Materials needed

- a case study written up on flip chart or on individual papers for each group;
- flip-chart paper and pens.

Methods used

- small group discussions;
- case studies;
- plenary discussions.

Steps

A. DEFINING COMMUNITY AND COMMUNITY PROJECTS

1. The facilitator introduces the session and relates it to the previous sessions, and gives the objectives and overview of activities.
2. The participants are asked to define, in small group discussion 'What is a community?' and 'What is a community project?'
3. Each group posts its written definition on the wall and a discussion is conducted on each question in turn, combining the small-group definitions.
4. Some consensus is reached on a whole-group definition.
5. The learning points from this activity are summarized by the group.

---

1. Adapted from a training session devised by the participants from Kenya.

B. DEFINING COMMUNITY INVOLVEMENT

1. The facilitator introduces the topic within the circle of seated participants by holding on to one end of a ball of string and tossing the ball to a participant opposite who pulls the string tight and in turn names a participant and throws the ball of string on. This continues until about half of the participants are holding the string and a net has been formed.

2. The facilitator then asks the participants to lift and lower the net and to watch what happens. The following questions are asked and discussed:
   - What do you see happening to this net (project)?
   - Why do you think this is so?
   - How do you feel being involved in holding up this net (as part of the community in which this net project is established)?
   - How do you feel not being involved in holding up the net (as part of the community in which this project is established)?
   - What can we do about this when establishing a community-based project or programme?

3. The learnings from this activity are discussed and summarized by the group.

C. THE CASE STUDY

1. The facilitator presents the case study to the plenary.

2. The participants convene in learning groups to discuss the case study.

3. Each group then gives feedback on the case study in turn and there is a plenary discussion on the problems and underlying causes and possible solutions.

4. The facilitator asks the group for concluding comments on the subject (key points) and adds in any further points required.

Key learning points on the community and community projects

1. A community is a group of people sharing common interests, goals and norms, such as a village, a religious congregation, a group of small-business owners, the education community, the early childhood community.

2. A community of people may live in the same geographic area, for example a village, or be widespread for example the community of a specific religion or church which is spread over several villages and towns, and indeed countries.

3. A geographic community may include people with similar or quite different cultural norms, practices, beliefs and language. All the people in the community may not thus feel committed to the same project, because they may have different priorities; for instance, one group of people may be

committed to and working towards the aims of a political party, another to the rights and needs of the aged within the community, another to the establishment of farming co-operatives, another to the rights of the female children in education, others to health and still others to early childhood development.

4. A community project is any activity undertaken by a community for its own welfare and development, in which the community is involved in the activity's inception, planning, implementation and evaluation. In this sense, the activity is endorsed by and owned by the community.

5. A community may be mobilized by:
   - creating awareness;
   - organizing the people in the community to assess and prioritize needs;
   - helping the members of the community to make a list of local resources;
   - providing technical and project management training.

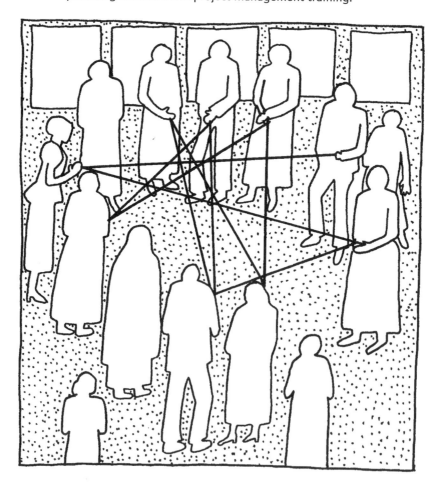

THE KOKUNGU CASE STUDY

The Kokungu Community is situated in the Coast Province of Kenya. The community has a population of about 2,500. Land productivity in Kokungu is low owing to erratic rainfall, soil erosion, high population pressure and poor farming methods. The people of Kokungu suffer from various problems as a result. In 1987 there was an acute cholera outbreak followed by measles and malaria. Many children and adults suffered.

The Member of Parliament for Kokungu approached Saidia, a funding agency, to assist the people. He told the agency that the major problems were ignorance, poverty and lack of health services.

Saidia agreed to help the people of Kokungu. They paid a visit to Kokungu and selected two sites on which to drill two wells. The wells were drilled and pumps installed. They were handed over to the Member of Parliament during an elaborate ceremony nine months later.

The people used each for about three months and eventually the pumps broke down and other complications arose. They sent a message to the Member of Parliament informing him of these problems and, in the meanwhile, abandoned the well and reverted to drawing water from the unprotected sources they had used earlier.

The wells have not been repaired up to now and parts of the pumps have been stolen.

Saidia also initiated a programme to improve child nutrition in the area. They did this by training the mothers how to make groundnut cakes which they could then feed to their children regularly. These cakes easily found a market beyond Kokungu and so helped the people to earn some income. During the period of training, Saidia supplied the groundnuts. At the end of the training period they did an evaluation and found that the mothers had learned how to make the cakes very well and that the children loved the cakes.

Saidia went away satisfied. After Saidia left, however, the supply of groundnuts dried up because Saidia had always provided the groundnuts. Women in the village ceased to make the cakes.

Questions

Why did the water and cakes projects fail?

How far did the community become involved in each project?

What would you do differently to ensure the projects succeed?

5. Homeless children[1]

Objectives

- to explore the causes and effects of separation from families and the community context of homelessness among children;
- to look at possible action to be taken by early childhood workers for children at risk or homeless.

Materials needed

- photographs and pictures of homeless children and children at risk of becoming homeless;
- flip-chart paper and pens.

Methods used

In plenary and small groups.

Steps

1. The facilitator introduces the topic by putting the pictures on the wall for everyone to look at while walking around (gallery walk).

2. The participants discuss what they observe in the pictures. The facilitator asks whether they have had experience of these sights in their own areas and, in particular, what ages the children are and what they think are the essential differences between the children in these pictures and other children. The topic and the purpose of the session are then announced.

3. Each small group discusses one of the following questions:
    - What do you think causes children to become separated or alienated from their families and to become homeless?
    - What do you think the effects on the children are? How would children feel about being separated and react?
    - How do homeless and 'familyless' children survive?
    - What do you think the effects on the families are?
    - What are the effects on the community in which the child lives?

---

1. Adapted from a training session devised by the participants from Ethiopia.

4. Each group reports to the plenary and participants add in points in general discussion.

5. The groups then discuss whether there is a role that early childhood development programmes and workers can play in prevention and alleviation of the phenomenon of street children and, if so, what it might involve. A list of achievable steps to take is made and shared with the group.

6. A synthesis of the learnings from this session is made.

Watch points

1. The underlying assumptions we hold about homeless children need to be clarified, whether they are perceived as 'less than' other children or as children challenged by their circumstances to survive.

2. It is important to establish in the beginning whether or not the phenomenon of homeless children is relevant to early childhood (this may entail revisiting the age span for early childhood in policy and practice).

3. This session plan can be adapted as an orientation activity to the discussion of children challenged in many different ways by their circumstances, for example through disability or poverty.

Key learning points on homeless children

1. The Convention on the Rights of the Child states that all children have the right to a home and a family life.

2. Homeless children have the same basic physical needs for food, shelter, love and security as all children as well as the same developmental needs. These needs are not all met in the circumstances in which they live. Homeless children have special needs in order to survive and to grow, as well as special education needs.

3. Children who are served in existing early childhood programmes are usually living in the family unit. They and their families may need support in order to remain as a family unit.

4. Children who are already homeless may not be served by any early childhood programme. The way in which programmes are devised needs to take into consideration the specific needs and skills that homeless children have.

5. The phenomenon of homelessness among children has many causes including poverty, joblessness, war, violence and famine that may lead to stress and may lead to child abuse, abandonment, homelessness and the break-up of families.

6. The effects of separation from the family unit and homelessness are extremely stressful for the child who has to survive by using all available resources and by any means at his or her disposal, whether or not they are considered by the community to be 'legal' or suitable.

7. The effect on the parents will also include great stress since parents love their children and want the best for them, but are prevented from doing so by the adverse circumstances noted above.

8. The effects of homelessness on the community may include strain on the health, economic, education and justice systems. There will also be a need to focus on underlying causes. Therefore long- and short-term solutions and programmes need to be aimed at eradicating the causes and alleviating the effects of homelessness.

6. Reflections

Objectives

To reflect critically on the learnings of the sessions on the community context
of early childhood development.

Materials needed

Paper and pens.

Methods used

- individual work, small groups and plenary discussions;
- voting procedure using stickers.

Steps

1. The facilitator invites participants to comment on the:
    - content of the sessions in this section;
    - process devised by the facilitators to achieve the objectives.

2. All points are written down by the facilitators.

3. Participants discuss points which need clarification or debate and plans are
    made to address points in later sessions as required.

Watch points

This session needs to be lively and short so that the day ends on an active and
dynamic note.

Purpose

> to integrate method with content in designing training sessions
> to explore positive ways of giving and receiving feedback
> to build a set of guidelines for self- and peer-evaluation of facilitators

Training sessions

(TIMINGS ARE APPROXIMATE)

1. Introduction
    (30 MINS)

2. Integrating method with content
    (2 HRS 30 MINS)

3. Giving and receiving feedback
    (1 HR)

4. Designing and presenting a training session
    (A FULL DAY)

5. Synthesizing our experiences in training
    (1 HR 30 MINS)

6. Reflections
    (1 HR)

CHAPTER 6

Planning, action and reflection

1. Introduction

Objective

- to reincorporate the group for this section;
- to generate some ideas for warming-up or ice-breaking activities.

Preparation

The facilitator asks volunteers to prepare a short activity to introduce this section.

Materials needed

Flip-chart paper and pens.

Method used

Individual work within the plenary.

Steps

1. Everyone sits in a circle. The facilitator welcomes everyone and asks the volunteer group to present their activity with the group as an icebreaker or warming-up activity.

2. The participants are asked to comment on the activity as an ice-breaker and to suggest other activities they have used successfully with groups.

3. A summary of key points about the use of introductory warming-up activities is made by asking participants first to talk with a partner and then to give points one pair at a time to the plenary.

4. The facilitator asks the participants for any thoughts on the previous day's programme that they may like to air in plenary.

5. The agenda for the day is given.

Watch point

Keep this session short and lively.

Key learning points on warming-up activities

1. The purpose of warming-up activities is to energize participants and to focus their attention on the following activity or part of the programme.

2. Warming-up activities can be used at the beginning of a session or day to introduce a topic.

3. They can also be used during sessions and between activities to revitalize the group by giving a change of pace or texture. This is particularly useful when the participants have just completed a long and complicated activity, or after a seated discussion, and particularly after a plenary session.

4. Warm-ups help participants to renew their concentration because they are short, active and fun.

5. They must be well-prepared and thought-out, and preferably be able to be related in some way to the content of the sessions under discussion; for example, a warming-up activity about names and their meanings would lead to a discussion on the importance of getting to know each other before meaningful work can be undertaken in a group.

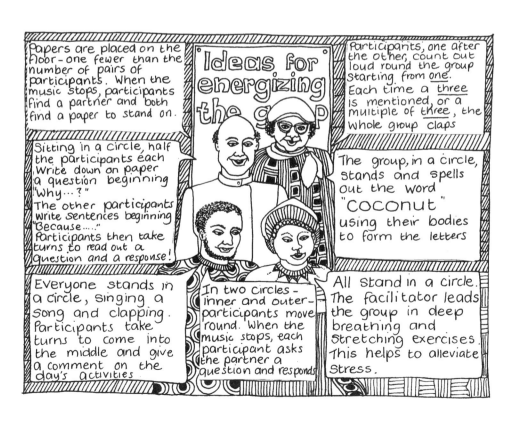

6. The facilitator can prepare specific warm-ups for the group beforehand as part of the preparation for the training event. Other warm-ups can be used whenever the facilitator sees the need for a change of pace and concentration among participants. Once the participants have got to know each other and feel relaxed in the group, individuals can be asked to volunteer to plan a warm-up for the group.

7. The warm-ups can be related to either the content of the training event or the next activity or session, or to the process of forming and maintaining the group.

8. The type of group and the mood of the group need to be taken into consideration when planning what types of warm-up to present: for instance, some groups may like and respond well to singing games while others may not. Some groups may need to discuss the relevance of warm-ups and whether or not they are a waste of time.

2. Integrating method with content

Objectives

To make more explicit:
- the link between the curriculum and participatory methods;
- the importance of having a strong knowledge base (key learning points) for any area of the early childhood development curriculum.

Materials needed

Flip-chart and pens.

Methods used

Pairs, small groups and plenary discussions.

Steps

1. The facilitator introduces the session by saying:
   'Part of the task of the facilitator is to integrate method and content in our training work and in applying method to content. We have all had experience in attempting to do this in our work and we need to draw on this so that we can structure our knowledge and build on our strengths. We need also to build on the guidelines we are developing for facilitators.'

2. In pairs, the participants discuss the ways in which they have integrated this participatory method in day-to-day training.

3. These ideas are given in plenary by participants telling everyone what their partner has said.

4. The facilitator asks for synthesizing sentences from the group, which are recorded on a flip-chart.

5. Leading on from some of the points made above, participants brainstorm the curriculum areas that they work with daily and a list is generated in the plenary group.

6. In small groups of four or five, participants:
   (a) choose one of the areas above;
   (b) define the key learning points which would emerge from the session(s) planned for this area;
   (c) think about the experiential participatory methods that could be applied to an area or areas of key learning;
   (d) plan a session based on one of these areas defining key learning points and possible activities or tasks for eliciting the learning points; and
   (e) display all the key learning areas and the activity plans for reading in a gallery walk.

7. The participants read the key learning areas displayed and each group asks for points of clarification and additions from the plenary on the key learning areas they have devised.

8. The facilitator asks for a summary of the learning points on the activity from the participants.

Watch point

It is often difficult to get hold of external resources in order to develop key learning points. Some resources noted at the back of the manual are available from the organizations involved in the Joint Training Initiative, UNICEF, Bernard van Leer Foundation, UNESCO, etc.

Key learning points on integrating method with content

1. People have a great deal of knowledge that needs to be brought out and then built on. This is called internal knowledge.

2. There needs to be very careful preparation of the key knowledge needed in an area before a training session is presented. This is called external knowledge; it may be found in people, books, videos and other resources. Knowledge about each stage of development of the child is important.

3. We begin by working with people's experiences and build on this. This is called the participatory experiential method. The conventional method of training works the other way round.

4. When using participatory experiential methods, the facilitator first finds out what knowledge the participants have and then builds on this.

5. When using the participatory method, it is important to remember that good knowledge of the subject under discussion is necessary. This means that the facilitator needs to prepare ahead by finding out through reading and discussion with colleagues and specialists in the subject. This advance preparation can also be done by a volunteer participant.

6. The facilitator can prepare ahead to a large extent, but needs to be flexible about what happens during the session.

7. The activities should be designed to help the participants to bring out the key learning points of the area under discussion (using their internal knowledge first). The facilitator then needs to be prepared to add in as necessary (using external knowledge).

8. When using these methods, the facilitator has to identify the appropriate method and moment to inject external knowledge – either orally or with a handout or pictures of some sort. This is called topping up on people's knowledge.

9. The facilitator needs to make sure that a summing up or synthesis of the learning points occurs at the end of the session. This summary is based on the outcomes expected during the planning stage and also what has emerged during the session (combining internal with external knowledge).

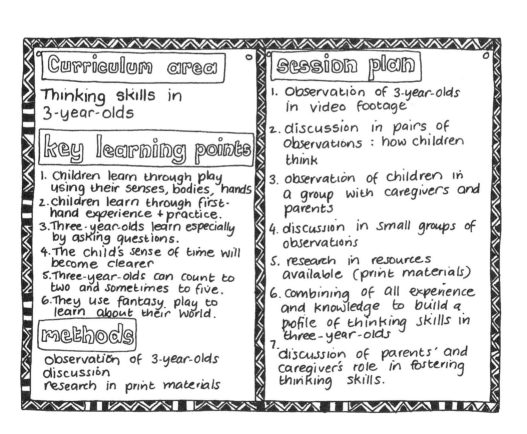

Curriculum area

Thinking skills in 3-year-olds

key learning points

1. Children learn through play using their senses, bodies, hands
2. children learn through first-hand experience + practice.
3. Three-year-olds learn especially by asking questions.
4. The child's sense of time will become clearer
5. Three-year-olds can count to two and sometimes to five.
6. They use fantasy play to learn about their world.

methods

observation of 3-year-olds
discussion
research in print materials

session plan

1. Observation of 3-year-olds in video footage
2. discussion in pairs of observations : how children think
3. observation of children in a group with caregivers and parents
4. discussion in small groups of observations
5. research in resources available (print materials)
6. combining of all experience and knowledge to build a profile of thinking skills in three-year-olds
7. discussion of parents' and caregiver's role in fostering thinking skills.

3. Giving and receiving feedback

Objectives

- to develop guidelines for giving and receiving feedback from colleagues and participants;
- to look at the implications for training, training of trainers and working with adults.

Preparation needed

Facilitators prepare a role play showing how <u>not</u> to give feedback, for example accusations, sulking, criticizing the person and not the action.

Methods used

- role play (two minutes only);
- plenary discussion.

Steps

1. The facilitators present the role play on negative feedback and then ask the participants the following questions which are answered in plenary.
   - What do you see happening here?
   - What do you think the effects are likely to be?

2. The facilitators at this point debrief on their own feelings about role playing this negative feedback.

3. In small groups of three the participants quickly develop concrete guidelines for giving feedback positively.

4. The facilitators ask for points in plenary which are written down on a flip-chart.

5. A volunteer pair is asked to present a role play showing the use of some of these points.

6. The plenary is asked for the implications of these learning outcomes on their own training and work in general.

7. The accompanying grid is given to the participants for noting points about the sessions that they observe for the later session on developing guidelines.

Watch point

Ensure that there is time to debrief for each role-playing group so that the roles are not confused with real-life roles.

Key learning points on giving and receiving feedback

1. Giving and receiving feedback is important for developing teamwork and a high quality of facilitation skills.

2. It needs to be done in the spirit of the values and norms developed by the participants, in other words, with respect for each person, with sensitivity and with openness.

3. More is learnt from feedback if we listen carefully to the feelings expressed and:
    *   do not try to defend our behaviour;
    *   do not attempt to give reasons about why we acted in that way.

    One cannot argue with feelings. If individuals feel bored or irritated or humiliated, it is no good telling them that 'they ought not to feel that way'. Each individual is the expert on his or her own feelings. Only by listening carefully to an individual's analysis of what caused those feelings can a facilitator learn how to avoid boring, irritating or humiliating other people.

4. An individual receiving feedback has the right to decide when he or she has had enough for the time being.

5. An individual who receives negative feedback should remember that different people react differently to different behaviour. He or she may like to check how others feel. If only one person reacted negatively, he or she may decide to do nothing about it, but if the majority felt that way, then it is important to try to change that behaviour.

6. Some guidelines for giving and receiving feedback could include the following:
    *   ensuring that there is first an opportunity for self-reflection, for example asking what the participant sees as the strengths and then adding those observed strengths;
    *   giving an opportunity for the person or group to state what they perceive to be the challenges (or weaknesses) and then adding any others;
    *   when giving criticism ensuring that the actions are challenged rather than the personalities or characters of the people involved and first asking why that particular action was taken before condemning it;
    *   remaining calm and listening actively, repeating back to the participant any negative feelings you may perceive, such as 'You are feeling angry about this' so that the person can correct any misperceptions or clarify feelings. Paraphrasing what is said to ensure clarity.

Recording observations of training sessions

Helpful ideas	Problems and challenges

4. Designing and presenting a training session

Objective

To design a forty-five-minute training session for presentation and review by the group by synthesizing internal and external knowledge about planning and presenting a training session.

Materials needed

Materials should be made available for the groups to use as they are needed.

Methods used

Small-group work.

Steps

1. The facilitator introduces the task as one leading on from the previous session, building on the participants' internal knowledge of planning and presenting training sessions as well as on the knowledge gained from this training event.

2. The session outline used in this training event is given to the participants on which to base their planning.

3. Each group chooses its topic from those generated previously and develops it to present to the plenary.

4. Roles are allocated to the group members for the presentation of the session:
   - facilitators;
   - helpers;
   - facilitator for the self-evaluation and group evaluation reflection session (thirty minutes immediately after the presentation of the session).

5. The group then presents the training session to the plenary for forty-five minutes.

6. Immediately after this, the group debriefs itself by giving a self-appraisal of its session and then chairs a thirty-minute plenary session, asking the plenary to comment on the session.

7. A plenary reflection session is held when all groups have made their presentations on the whole experience.

Watch points

1. It is important to keep strictly to the timetable in order to prevent the session from dragging. It may be useful to appoint a timekeeper for each session.

2. Remind participants when giving feedback to discuss actions rather than persons.

Key learning points on designing and presenting a training session

When planning a session for presentation, the following issues need to be taken into consideration:
- Who will anchor or chair the session and exactly what roles will be played by each facilitator in the team?
- Prior preparation of charts and materials is necessary so that the session flows smoothly and quickly without being held up by the facilitators being perceived as disorganized and fumbling or not working as a team.
- What handouts or topping up needs to be given and how? Who will prepare this?
- How will the session outcomes be documented?

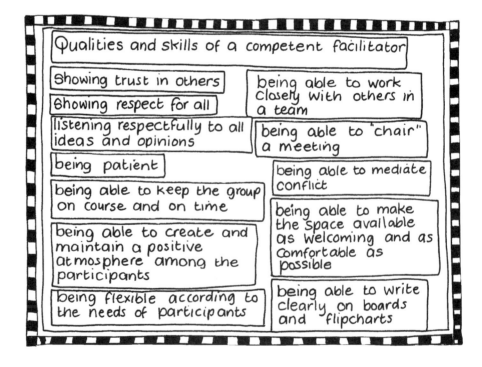

Qualities and skills of a competent facilitator

Showing trust in others

Showing respect for all

listening respectfully to all ideas and opinions

being patient

being able to keep the group on course and on time

being able to create and maintain a positive atmosphere among the participants

being flexible according to the needs of participants

being able to work closely with others in a team

being able to "chair" a meeting

being able to mediate conflict

being able to make the space available as welcoming and as comfortable as possible

being able to write clearly on boards and flipcharts

Designing a training session

Title

Time

Objectives

Materials needed

Methods used

Steps

Watch points

Key learning points

5. Synthesizing our experiences in training

Objectives

Working from the experience of practising and observing facilitation:
* to identify best practice;
* to build a set of guidelines/actions for self-reflection and evaluation that can be used by trainers in both their own self-evaluation as well as guides to observing and monitoring the skills of trainers at the field levels.

Materials needed

Flip-chart: areas of operation for trainers:
* planning/design;
* facilitation;
* review.

Methods used

Individual, pair and small-group work.

Steps

1. The facilitator introduces the topic by saying that everyone has seen extremely good practices in the facilitation practice sessions: each group demonstrated some excellent models for training/facilitation. These need to be discussed, collated and used as self-evaluation guidelines, working from concrete practice (using the information gathered in the observation grid as well).

2. As individuals, write down guidelines for:
   * planning a training event;
   * designing a training session;
   * facilitating training sessions;
   * reflecting on and evaluating training.

3. In pairs, discuss, clarify and add to these guidelines.

4. Small groups are formed, each taking one category and developing a set of guidelines for that category.

5. All lists are then put up on the wall for silent reading.

6. Participants then raise points and additions in plenary discussion.

7. The facilitator asks for suggestions on how guidelines developed from this could be used by the participants.

Watch points

1. The guidelines should be as concrete, observable and measurable as possible.

2. Having pre-prepared flip-charts helps to focus the groups on the practical outcomes required in this activity.

Key learning points

1. Self-evaluation questionnaires that are developed by the participants themselves are extremely useful in focusing on what is considered by all to be good practice. Standards for facilitation are developed that can be used by facilitators to gauge their own performance and that of their colleagues.

2. The questionnaires developed by the participants of the Joint Training Initiative are to be found in Chapter 10.

6. Reflections: implications for practice

Objective

To reflect on the steps taken by the facilitators in the previous sessions from the point of view of a facilitator.

Materials needed

Flip-chart paper divided into two columns:
- What happened?
- What was the effect?

Methods used

Pairs discussion and plenary discussion.

Steps

1. The facilitator introduces the session by referring to the programme listing the four sessions on 'Planning, action and evaluation' and asks the question 'Putting yourself into the position of a facilitator for this section:
   - 'What did you notice the trainers do to facilitate and orchestrate these sessions and outcomes?
   - 'What was the effect of each of these actions (negative and positive)?'

2. The participants are paired and each pair is given one of the sessions to discuss for a few minutes.

3. The facilitator asks the pairs to name the actions taken by the trainers during the session, and what effect it had on learning. The whole group is asked to add other points. Each of the sessions is broadly but critically analysed in this way and points are written up on the flip chart as they are given.

4. The points are collated for action the following day as necessary.

5. The session is closed.

Watch points

1. Ensure that this session is well timed so that a fast pace is maintained; it is important that broad overviews are given at this stage and that participants are able to appraise performance critically with a view to facilitating the sessions themselves.

2. Make certain that any points that need to be acted upon by the facilitators are addressed as soon as possible and a report on progress given to the participants the following day. This serves to build trust further between the facilitators and the participants.

3. It may take some time for the participants to be able to give a critical evaluation of the facilitators' performance; a fairly high level of trust needs to be established in order to be able to do this.

Key learning points on reflection

1. The skill of critical evaluation is an important aspect of learning and teaching, and life, that needs to be nurtured in all people from the young child to the adult.

2. Reflection needs to be done in a way that does not harm the person involved. It should be directed at actions rather than at persons.

3. It is useful to structure the way in which the analysis is conducted before starting a topic so that it can be approached in a systematic way, with the optimum opportunity to learn coming from the experience.

Purpose

> to discuss critically the ways of influencing policy and raising awareness for early childhood development
> to develop a profile of a change agent in this process and strategies for coping with this role

Training sessions

(TIMINGS ARE APPROXIMATE)

1. Introduction: communication

(30 MINS)

2. Influencing policy and raising awareness

(3 HRS)

3. Convincing donors

(1 HR 30 MINS)

4. Influencing politicians

(1 HR 30 MINS)

5. Setting up task teams

(1 HR 15 MINS)

6. Being an agent of change

(1 HR 15 MINS)

7. Reflections

(30 MINS)

1. Introduction: communication

Objectives

- to introduce the sessions on influencing policy and raising awareness;
- to illustrate the importance of listening to others through non-verbal behaviour (body language).

Materials needed

- pens and sheets of blank paper;
- objectives and the agenda for the section written on a flip-chart.

Methods used

Pair work and plenary.

Steps

1. The facilitator welcomes everyone to this section and asks each person to choose a partner and to sit facing the partner across a table.

2. Each pair receives one sheet of paper and one pen and is asked to put the paper between them so that they can draw a picture on the paper both holding the pen.

3. The facilitator asks the participants <u>not</u> to speak at all from this time onwards, until the task is complete.

4. The participants are asked to <u>hold the pen together</u> and to draw <u>in silence</u> a picture of a child and an adult together outside a house standing next to a tree.

5. Once this is done, the pair must both sign the picture together and then post it on the wall (<u>all still in silence</u>).

6. The facilitator then invites everyone to look at the pictures that have been drawn and to comment on them.

7. Once everyone has commented, the facilitator asks the participants to draw out and summarize (synthesize) the learnings from the activity.

8. The objectives and the agenda for the section are given.

Watch points

1. Ensure that the pairs carry out this activity in silence. It is important that all instructions for the activity are understood clearly before the activity is begun.

2. The activity should be conducted in a light-hearted and lively manner.

Key learning points on communication

1. Good communication consists of clear statements and a clear understanding of what is being said, both verbally and non-verbally.

2. Non-verbal communication needs to be understood in terms of the cultural background of the persons involved in the conversation.

3. In order to be quite clear about exactly what is being communicated, it is important when listening to ask for clarification, or to feed back to the speaker one's understanding of what has been said.

4. It is also important for the speaker to make sure that what he or she is saying is correctly perceived by the listener. Ways of asking for clarification include:

   'My understanding of what you are saying is that . . .'

   'How do you feel about this?'

2. Influencing policy and raising awareness

Objectives

- to explore: why it is important to influence early childhood policy; whom to influence; what arguments will sway policy; and how to influence strategy;
- to plan a policy-influencing strategy in each area or organization.

Materials needed

Booklets and information on early childhood policy, for example, from Save the Children Foundation, UNICEF, UNESCO, Bernard van Leer Foundation, and other early childhood development advocacy materials.

Methods used

- individual, pair and group work;
- role plays.

Steps

The facilitator explains the idea of the wider role of the trainer as an advocate of change, the need for policy work as part of the wider Initiative and the purpose of the session.

1. Why is it important to influence policy?

   (a) Individuals are asked to each write down one reason why they think it is important for early childhood development facilitators to influence early childhood policy.

   (b) In groups they then share these thoughts and combine their individual statements into one strong rationale for influencing policy.

   (c) Groups then share them in plenary.

   (d) The facilitator adds external knowledge as required.

2. Who to be influenced?

   The participants discuss together in pairs who needs to be influenced and then in plenary make up a list of whom to influence at the local, national, regional and international levels.

3. What arguments will sway policy?

    (a) Each of the categories of policy-makers is allocated to a group of participants.

    (b) Each group analyses what sort of message will most likely convince the policy-maker to support early childhood development.

    (c) Each group then makes a list of the key statements within this message.

    (d) These lists are reported back in plenary.

4. How to influence policy (strategies or methods to use)

    (a) A chart with the title 'How to Influence Policy' is displayed and participants are invited to write up ways they have used or heard used to influence people.

    (b) Everybody then reads these and adds to the chart or asks for clarification.

    (c) Each group then refocuses on its own policy-maker category and develops a role play to depict how an early childhood development facilitator would advocate for changes in early childhood policy.

    (d) The role plays are presented. The role-players first debrief and then comments are sought from the large group on the strategy and techniques used to influence policy. (Did they work or not? Why?)

    (e) In plenary, general lessons and insights about influencing policy are shared and key learning points are synthesized.

5. Area or organization strategies

    (a) Area or organization teams get together to write down a draft description of the strategy each will use to mobilize support from the various categories of policy-maker in the area for the early childhood development training Initiative.

    (b) The following aspects are included:

    * support needed from agencies;
    * links to national policies and declarations;
    * steering committees (task teams) and links to a national steering committee;
    * focusing on the few key policy-makers that will make a big difference.

    (c) These draft ideas are kept for future reference in the session on developing a plan of action.

Watch points

As facilitators, participants are relatively new to policy work and may need support in exploring this issue. This session also has many activities, requiring tight time management. Ensure that there is time for a break during the session, for instance between Activity 4 and Activity 5.

Key learning points on influencing policy and raising awareness

1. Why it is important to place early childhood development on local and national agendas:

   (a) Holistic early childhood intervention programmes seem to have a long-term impact in the areas of personality development and motivation (self-esteem). This means that there may be long-term outcomes such as lower expenditure on special education, less drug addiction, lower delinquency rates, higher incomes and decreased use of welfare services.

   (b) Holistic early childhood programmes address not only cognitive development but also socio-emotional and physical development, including nutrition and health. This comprehensive approach positively affects contributions in later life, for example better social skills, greater competence, and a healthier population with an ability to work more productively and less likelihood of becoming a drain on health and welfare systems.

   (c) Investing in the education of women – especially mothers – and girls through the parent and community involvement aspects of early childhood development can result in a significant decline in infant mortality rates and an increase in health as well as an increase in confidence and self-esteem.

   (d) The long-term impact of early childhood programmes on later achievement in school can include being in the right grade at the right age, staying at school longer and being more likely to find employment on leaving school.

   (e) Early childhood programmes can help disadvantaged children to gain cognitive, language and socio-emotional skills.

   (f) Early childhood programmes can be a springboard for community development.

   (g) The cost-effectiveness of holistic early childhood programmes that include nutrition, health and education for parents as well as for children can be greater than for these programmes when they are run separately from one another.

2. Whom do we need to influence?

   (a) Locally:
   - parents and family members;
   - community groups, for instance civic associations;
   - community leaders, for instance chiefs, religious leaders, traditional early childhood trainers and grass-roots workers in the fields of development, social work and health;
   - employers and trade unions;
   - local government;
   - non-government and community-based organizations;
   - teachers in primary and secondary schools.

(b) Nationally:
  • politicians and political parties;
  • administrators and state departments;
  • institutions, for instance research and training institutions;
  • mass media;
  • teachers' and health workers' unions;
  • Ministries of Women's Affairs, Community Development and Health and Welfare, etc.;
  • donor agencies and non-governmental organizations.

3. Ways in which we can influence people:
  • through meetings with influential people;
  • holding seminars and rallies (mass meetings);
  • distributing pamphlets and posters;
  • news coverage in newspapers and magazines most commonly read;
  • radio and television programmes;
  • community drama groups;
  • whatever ways each community uses to spread information and generate discussion.

4. Guidelines for influencing policy
  (a) Be **very well prepared** before going to any meeting with high-level people:
    • have all statistics and facts together;
    • have a written report/proposal for any ministers, politicians, business people, etc.;
    • have a good clear knowledge of economic factors showing how early childhood development will benefit the country, business and later education economically;
    • know how much the programme will cost and who has been approached for funding (parents, communities, local government, businesses, donors, central government, etc.);
    • have a good clear knowledge of the partnerships in early childhood and counterpart funders for early childhood.
  (b) Find an intermediary person to introduce or support you for meetings with ministries, etc.
  (c) Use media if they are available, for example videos, slides, photographs.
  (d) Make sure that you discuss the things that high-level officials, etc., will be interested in. They will probably be more interested in the economic, educational and health benefits of early childhood programmes than in discussing play equipment or classroom activities, etc. Be prepared for all types of questions. Try to work out what they are likely to be before you go to the meeting. Make sure that you can answer the questions.

(e) Target different ministries and groups so that you get some liaison between them, for example, the Ministry of Education and the Ministries of Health, Women's Affairs, Finance, etc.

(f) Make sure that you show respect to the persons that you meet according to custom (you may need to find out what the custom is).

5. Some guidelines for raising community awareness about early childhood

(a) When addressing community groups, make sure that you **listen** very carefully indeed to the needs of the families in the community and encourage people to make up their own minds about a possible plan of action. (Lecturing to a group will not convince them!)

(b) First of all, before any meetings are held, find out who the key people are in that community (the 'gatekeepers') and talk to them, ask for advice and guidance on how best to go about planning a meeting, etc.

(c) Make sure that the message that you give to the group is relevant to the needs of the community (for example, it may be about the real problems of looking after children daily when the parents are away and there is little food, etc.).

(d) Make sure that you show respect to the group according to the custom of that group.

3. Convincing donors[1]

Objective

To develop strategies for convincing donors to support early childhood programmes.

Materials needed

A pre-prepared role play using participants as players.

Two early childhood training co-ordinators try to convince the donor in a meeting with the district education officer that the donor should finance a new early childhood development training programme. Neither party has any prior information about the programmes, the co-facilitators are ill-prepared and the meeting is chaotic.

Methods used

Role play, group discussion and plenary.

Steps

1. The facilitators introduce the activity by announcing the role play and the characters in it.

2. After the presentation, the participants in pairs discuss:
   • what they saw happening in the role play;
   • what they would do next if they were the two co-facilitators;
   • how they should have handled the meeting to get the results they wanted.

3. Each pair then joins with another pair to discuss their responses and takes a turn to give a response to each question until all the points are exhausted.

4. Debate on points is taken as needed. The facilitators ask for summary points and the learning points are 'banked' for the session on planning later.

5. Each person is asked to reflect on this session in one sentence.

---

1. Adapted from a training session designed and presented by the participants from Zimbabwe.

Watchpoints

When asking participants to prepare a role play to introduce a session, be sure to give them all the information they will need to devise a short drama that is to the point and entertaining.

Key learning points on convincing donors

1. When approaching potential donors for funding, make sure that a lot of preparatory work has been done so that the donors, together with the local government officials, understand the purpose of the visit.

2. Find out what the donor policies and government policies are before asking for a meeting with them.

3. Be prepared for political and power rivalries. Use the proper channels in setting up a meeting and be sensitive to possible 'game-playing'.

4. Prepare the agenda clearly before the meeting and make sure that all parties have a copy well before the meeting.

5. Prepare the donor for involvement in the project from the beginning.

6. Discuss and clarify lines of communication within all role-playing organizations.

7. Make sure that details about proposed plans and budget are clarified and understood by all, so that donors know exactly what is being requested.

8. As each section of the project, for example the training event, is completed, give a verbal report to donors and the government department as soon as possible.

9. Prepare a comprehensive and legible report with an accompanying short executive summary within a fortnight and send it as soon as possible to the donors and other role-playing organizations.

10. When you send the report, send a summary report and covering letter asking for a debriefing meeting.

4. Influencing politicians[1]

Objectives

To assist participants to sensitize local leaders concerning issues of child survival and early childhood development and to begin to mobilize them towards plans of action.

Preparation and materials needed

- role play and flip-charts;
- local and comparative statistics on infant mortality, child health, fertility rates, maternal mortality rates, per capita income, etc.;
- chart showing the problem-analysis method;
- flip-charts and pens.

Methods used

Role play and group work.
The facilitators act out the parts of political leaders, a chairperson, heads of departments involved in children's affairs, non-governmental organizations and donor organizations.
All the participants play the role of the members of parliament.
The session is conducted as a workshop for politicians – the entire session is thus a role play.

Steps

1. The role play is staged without explanation or introduction by the facilitators who begin by opening a meeting of local leaders and asking the following question: 'What would be your reaction on finding that (state the numbers of children who die annually from preventable disease in the area) young children have been killed in a disaster in our area?'

2. Participants are asked to respond to this question in plenary.

3. The facilitator (who chairs the meeting) then states the number of young children who die each year in the country from poverty-related diseases and asks the 'local leaders' for their reaction.

---

1. Adapted from a training session prepared and presented by the participants from Malawi.

4. A plenary discussion is conducted on the causes of this.

5. A 'health representative' presents a comparative table of figures for the area and other areas and countries regarding the per capita income, infant mortality, total fertility rates and maternal mortality rate per 1,000 and asks for questions and comment from the plenary.

6. The 'Chair' presents a method of analysing problems and asks small district/regional/country groups to use the method to develop a feasible plan of action around the problem.

7. The 'Chair' asks for reports from each group and a plan of action is proposed for next steps by the group as a whole.

8. The 'Chair' closes the meeting.

9. The facilitators de-role themselves and debrief themselves on their role as local leaders. They then ask for reflections on the session by the participants.

10. Key learning points are summarized by the group and 'external knowledge' is added as necessary.

Watchpoints

1. This session, as well as being a training session involved with trainees on courses, is also an activity for working with politicians, donors, etc. It could be presented to all sectors of policy-makers.

2. When presenting this activity to community leaders, be very careful to follow up with an agreed set of actions and times in order to maintain interest in the subject with people who are extremely busy with many demands on their time and attention.

Key learning points on influencing local leaders

1. Most of the arguments given for the need for intervention are 'soft arguments' that will appeal to Ministers of Education and Health, Women and Children, but will not appeal to Ministers of Finance and Planning, who need to be presented with economic facts and figures. All have to be convinced, but especially the Ministry of Forestry, Agriculture, Mining, etc., which produce income. (The Ministry of Finance relies on these income-generating 'hard' ministries for funding for the ministries that do not generate income, such as Education, Health and Welfare, and they are extremely difficult to influence since there is so much demand put on them for funding.)

2. We need to give a table of figures that shows the impact of investment in education (economic evidence) at advocacy meetings of this nature. These figures can be found in most government departments and in publications by UNICEF and UNESCO within the country.

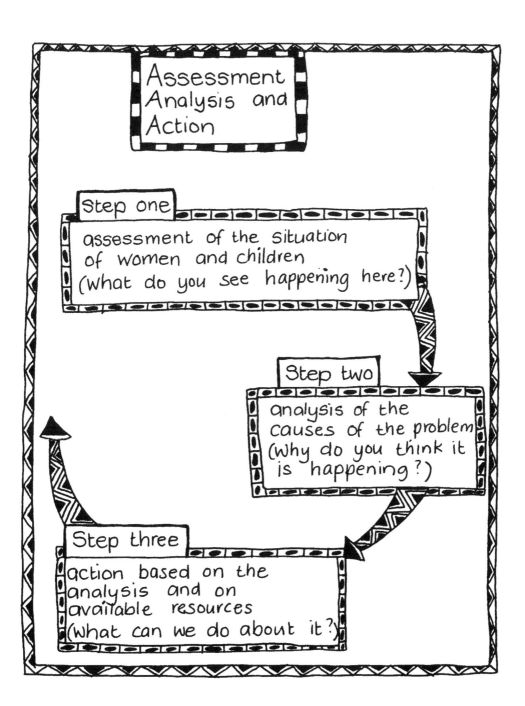

Assessment Analysis and Action

Step one
assessment of the situation of women and children
(what do you see happening here?)

Step two
analysis of the causes of the problem
(why do you think it is happening?)

Step three
action based on the analysis and on available resources
(what can we do about it?)

5. Setting up task teams[1]

Objective

To tackle some common problems and challenges in planning and setting up a task team on early childhood policy.

Materials needed

Flip-chart paper.

Methods used

Group work, case study, role play and plenary discussion.

Steps

1. The facilitator introduces the session and states the objectives.

2. The participants work in three groups on a case study each, using the Four Open Questions to analyse the problem and propose solutions.

3. The solutions to the challenges portrayed in the case study are presented to the plenary.

4. The group discusses key learnings from the session and banks information for the later session on plans of action.

Key learning points on setting up task teams

1. When setting up a task team it is important to have discussed, with a wide range of role players, the possible purpose and objectives of the team and the best ways of setting up the team.

2. Make sure that all relevant organizations are invited to attend the first meeting. Issue the invitation in good time together with a clear agenda for the meeting. It is useful to follow up on invitations as well to ensure that they have been received.

3. An interim Chair for the meeting is needed before the office bearers are elected to take the process further.

---

1. Adapted from a training session devised and presented by the participants from Uganda.

4. Some possible items for discussion at a first task team meeting might include:
   - reason for the meeting and need for a task team;
   - introduction of participants and their areas of operation;
   - identification of other role players for inclusion in the process;
   - a preliminary survey of needs of children and their families and current programmes;
   - identification of gaps in current programmes;
   - establishing norms and communication channels for the group and decisions on representation at further meetings;
   - objectives and tasks for the team and following meetings.

CASE STUDY ONE: TACKLING APATHY

A group of national early childhood facilitators is enthusiastic and ready to implement their new knowledge and skills in the participatory, experiential approach.

They write their report and hold several meetings.

They attempt to see the Assistant Commissioner for Education (in charge of basic education and early childhood development) but he is too busy to be seen.

Finally, after months, he gets a secondary-school-trained staff member to deal with the trainers, but this officer does not have much idea about early childhood development, nor any interest in it.

Task

Discuss and plan a role play to report on solutions to these problems.

CASE STUDY TWO: SETTING UP A TASK TEAM

The national early childhood facilitators have just completed a training-of-trainers course and are asked to set up a task team because of high expectations of key people in the Ministry of Education.

They have to decide on whom to include, and set up terms of reference and a work plan.

Task

Make a presentation for the ministry of the Plan of action you intend to take to ensure a successful task team on early childhood development.

CASE STUDY THREE: BUILDING A PARTNERSHIP FOR POLICY

The national early childhood facilitators want to create a first draft of a policy document for early childhood development, using the expertise of both the non-governmental organizations working for early childhood development and the relevant government departments in the area.

They want to do this by building a partnership between the non-governmental organizations working with early childhood development and the relevant government departments.

Neither the non-governmental organizations nor the government departments are very keen to do this.

Task

Propose ways of bringing these potential partners together.

6. Being an agent of change

Objectives

To examine the role of facilitator as a change agent and to develop responses to the challenges of this role.

Materials needed

- chart showing the change process, problem is identified, denial of the problem, resistance, anger, depression and acceptance;
- chart showing areas of control, influence and understanding:
  - control (participant has some control over this area),
  - influence (participant has some influence in this area),
  - understanding and appreciation (participant needs to understand and appreciate elements in this area).

Methods used

Group work and plenary discussion.

Steps

1. The facilitator restates the expectations of the Initiative as a whole for development in each region or district:
   - starting from where we are;
   - working from the needs of the country and the environment;
   - gradual (micro-)change rather than instant (mega-)change (community development principle).

2. The facilitator asks: 'How sure are you that this participatory and experiential method is genuinely a good method of working and is going to work in your region?'

3. The participants are asked to place themselves on a continuum from one end of the training space to the other; one end is for those who are 'completely sure that this method will not work' and the other end is for those who are 'completely sure that this method will work'.

4. The participants are asked to give random reasons for why they have placed themselves at particular points along the continuum.

5. The facilitator then explains that every change agent has an area of control and influence, and a wider set of elements that cannot be controlled but which must be recognized and appreciated if he or she is to become a competent change agent, and asks for comment on this idea.

6. In the light of the challenges posed for being an agent of change, the participants are asked in groups to develop a set of qualities and tasks for a change agent.

7. These are written on slips of paper and posted on the wall for everyone to read.

8. The points are categorized and discussion around them is taken in plenary.

9. Each participant then marks with a tick the area he or she feels most hopeful about and with a cross the area he or she feels most concerned about.

10. The main hopes and fears are identified, highlighted and summarized, and then banked for the sessions on plans of action later on.

11. The facilitator then states the challenge of the 'facilitator as agent of change' in the light of the comments about the continuum, and shows the diagram of the path of change and the way in which people react to change.

12. Each person makes a mark on the diagram where he or she feels represents present feelings about being an agent of change.

Key learning points about being an agent of change

1. The path of change shows the different stages through which people move when confronted with radical change in their lives.

2. People progress through these stages at different rates and in different ways (the path is very convoluted and long, and often turns back on itself).

3. People may remain stuck at a stage for a very long time and may even not progress beyond a stage.

4. They may also swing back and forth from one stage to another at times.

5. Each change agent has a very small circle of people with whom he or she works and over whom he or she has some control, for example those whom he or she supervises.

6. There is some possibility of functioning directly as an agent of change with this group in that plans of action can be developed and supervised with this group.

7. The circle of people whom the change agent can influence is far larger than that over which there is some control.

8. This circle can grow enormously as the change agent develops a greater knowledge of the early childhood development environment and the issues involved, knowledge of the people who need to be influenced and in particular knowledge of him- or herself (such as strengths and weaknesses).

9. The circle of influence is very much influenced in turn by the outer circle awareness and understanding of the environment – both external and internal (people's likes and dislikes, needs and wants).

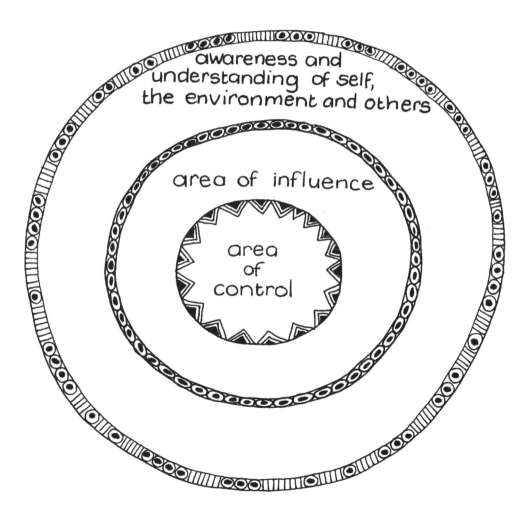

The human response to change

the stages we go through in coping with change

We reach a new contentment through the new order

We begin to be proactive and make positive plans for the future

We start to accept the change in a resigned sort of way

We either fight flight (flee) or freeze in the face of change

We start to grow used to the change in name only (same old system, new names)

We react to the change by denying it (shock, fear, disbelief, numbness)

a change occurs (a paradigm shift)

the old order and ways of doing things

Start here

the path we travel to get to a new contentment

7. Reflections

Objective

To reflect on the key learnings of the section on influencing policy and raising awareness for early childhood.

Materials needed

None.

Methods used

Individual and pair work in plenary.

Steps

1. The facilitator asks each participant to think quietly for a minute about the key learning of this section, to turn to a partner and discuss it.

2. Each participant then gives his or her partner's point to the plenary.

3. Participants are then asked as individuals to think about any aspect of the section that causes anxiety, to share this with the partner and for the partner to report back to the plenary.

4. Common threads are discovered and discussed as necessary.

5. The session ends with a five-word comment from each participant on being an agent of change.

Watch point

Ensure that this final session in the section is short, to the point and as upbeat as possible.

Purpose

> to develop plans of action for:
>   - a training cycle
>   - influencing policy and raising awareness
>   - evaluation

Training sessions

(TIMINGS ARE APPROXIMATE)

1. Introduction

    (30 MINS)

2. Planning a training cycle and planning for influencing
    policy

    (1 HR 30 MINS)

3. Planning for evaluation

    (1 HR)

4. Presentation of highlights

    (1 HR 30 MINS)

5. Planning time of about a day

    (4 TO 6 HRS)

CHAPTER 8

Making plans of action

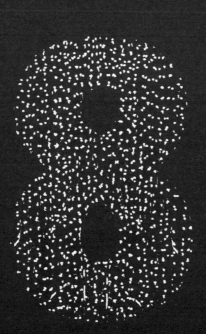

1. Introduction

Objective

To prepare for planning, training and advocacy programmes in the areas in which the participants live and work.

Steps

1. The facilitator welcomes everyone to the session on planning and restates the objectives and expectations for this training event. They are:
   - the training of facilitators,
   - influencing early childhood policy,
   in the area in which each participant lives and works.

2. The facilitator explains that for this planning activity each participant will be working at a different pace. Some will be continuing a process of training and policy-making that has already begun and others will be beginning the process from scratch.

3. Each team of participants works in a different environment and thus each plan of action will suit a particular set of circumstances. No two plans of action will be the same.

4. The framework for the plan of action covers the following areas:
   - training cycle;
   - influencing policy and raising awareness;
   - evaluation;
   - developing as a change agent.

Watch point

Make sure that the introduction is short, businesslike and to the point so that it marks a transition from the training to the planning phase of the training event.

2. Planning the training cycle and planning to influence policy

Objectives

- to reflect on the knowledge we have about the training cycle and to use it in starting to plan a training cycle for our area or region;
- to reflect on the knowledge we have about influencing policy and raising awareness, and to use it in starting to plan a training cycle for our area or region.

Materials needed

- a chart on the training cycle;
- planning charts for each group for planning the training cycle and influencing policy.

Methods used

Small groups, group-to-group discussion, plenary discussion.

Steps

1. Planning the training cycle
   (a) The facilitator reminds everyone of the steps in the training cycle.
   (b) The planning groups decide upon:
      - a broad training goal for the Initiative in the area or organization;
      - the specific objectives (or expected outcomes) for the training programme;
      - the first (concrete) steps to be taken to initiate the training cycle for the Initiative in the region.
   (c) The planning groups find a partner group to discuss their objectives and steps. The partner group asks questions for clarity and ensures that the proposed objectives, outcomes and steps are achievable.
   (d) In the plenary group, participants are invited to comment on their experiences so far in planning a training Initiative.
   (e) The facilitator points out that the process of planning has begun!

2. Planning to influence policy and raise awareness for early childhood
   (a) The participants then follow the same process in beginning to plan for influencing policy and raising awareness for early childhood in their areas or organizations.

(b) The planning charts are given out to each group and read and discussed, and all clarifications that need to be made are dealt with.

Watch points

1. It is important that participants be successful in planning a few small steps at a time and then to come back together to discuss and compare results and progress.

2. Participants may need more time than is expected to practise the art of planning achievable steps; ensure that everyone is quite clear about what is to be done in this activity.

3. Planning is to be done as a 'real life' activity. These plans will form the basis for the work to be done after the training event and for the assessment of its outcomes.

4. This process helps participants to confirm themselves and each other as competent planners.

5. Objectives should be achievable and measurable, and the steps should be designed in such a way that they are also achievable and lead on from one to the other in a logical sequence or chain.

6. The facilitators adopt the role during this session of consultants or advisers to the process and are on hand whenever participants require their support.

Early Childhood Training Initiative Plan of Action

Area of operation ....

Organization ....

Names of participants

....

....

....

1. Plans for the training cycle

(a) Analysis of the situation at present

194

(b) Key participants for training programmes

(c) Overall purpose of the training

(d) Plans for the training cycle

No.	Objectives for the year	Specific activities for the year

2. Influencing policy and raising awareness

(a) Analysis of the situation at present

(b) Key early childhood decision-makers

(c) Objectives for Year 1		
Target group	**Objective per target group**	**Key activities for the year**

3. Planning for evaluation

Objective

To help participants to plan a specific process for measuring the outcomes of the Initiative activities in their sphere of activity.

Materials needed

Chart showing the process of evaluation.

Methods used

Discussion in plenary.

Steps

1. The facilitator introduces this session by stating the purpose of the session and then asks the participants to discuss with a neighbour the purpose for evaluation in the first year and to give responses to the plenary.

2. The participants are then asked to discuss in small groups how they would best like to evaluate their progress in the Initiative using a participatory approach.

3. The groups discuss this and report to the plenary.

4. The facilitator then adds information to this by listing the components of this participative and qualitative approach:
   - Each area or organization will be treated as an individual case study.
   - Information will be gathered by the participants themselves in reports and observations.
   - An external evaluator will work with the participants themselves in gathering information and structuring it, using various instruments.

5. The participants then brainstorm the sort of information about the context and the learning that would be useful in assessing the impact of training and advocacy programmes.

6. A format for the evaluation plan is given to each team to read and discuss.

7. A question-and-answer time is held about the format and the whole evaluation plan.

8. The area or organizational groups then take the rest of the day and more if needed to plan all the training, advocacy and evaluation strategies, asking for assistance from other groups and the facilitators as they need it.

Watch points

1. It will take each team some time to complete this task. It is advisable to set aside at least a day for the full process of planning.

2. Much support for the process will need to be given. The idea of evaluation can be threatening, especially when our experiences of it in the past have been top-down and inspectoral rather than participative and formative.

3. Each completed plan will include both early childhood training-for-trainers plans and advocacy activities which will be easy to follow and to put into action.

4. As the participants go back to their places of work, they may need to modify these plans when they consult further with their own colleagues and the role players in the region. Flexibility should therefore be built into the process (including the plans for further consultation).

5. As each regional situation varies and as each participant has a different role in his or her work and area, so the plans will vary. Each plan will be unique.

Key learning points on evaluation

1. Evaluation is a key managerial activity that assists planners and facilitators to keep the project on track for the participants, and to influence policy and raise awareness for the project.

2. Evaluation is carried out for several groups, for instance:
   - the people in the project itself (participants and facilitators);
   - the local community (parents and families of children involved in early childhood programmes, etc.);
   - the sponsors (Department of Education, donor organizations, etc.);
   - community leaders, supporters, patrons, politicians and influential groups.

3. For an evaluation programme to be effective, the role players need to co-operate and work as a team. Evaluation is a collaborative exercise. It belongs to everyone concerned with a project. Only if people are involved will its outcomes be accepted and valued.

4. A team exercise in writing the history of the project can help to put the project in a more informed and sensitive setting. The setting of the project is important because each project will be unique according to its own particular environment and set of external and internal factors.

5. People are the richest source of information. By recording their stories, by interviewing them and by inviting them to share their knowledge with others we can learn how general trends affect personal lives and projects.

6. Do not collect information just for the sake of it. Always ask: 'Why are we asking these questions? What are we going to do with the answers?'
   The following sorts of records can be kept:
   - reports;
   - diaries;
   - minutes;
   - questionnaires;
   - interview reports.

7. The people within the project should be involved in the evaluation. An outsider could perhaps contribute an external viewpoint and more objectivity to the report.

8. Before starting the evaluation, plan how much time will be needed, as well as other costs such as travel and an external evaluator's time.

9. Make sure that records are accurate and carefully filed for use in evaluating the project. People will want to know that the evaluation is based on reliable facts and is valid.
   - Reliability means that the data genuinely reflect the situation in the project.
   - Validity means that the conclusions made in the evaluation are supported by the data in the report.

10. Before embarking on the evaluation, identify the issues to be studied first. Formulate questions to be asked around these issues so that exact data can be collected. Decide how the information is to be collected and from whom. Be sure that the questions are clear and give the type of answers you require.

11. You can use a written or interview questionnaire, a checklist, observation, informal interviews, etc., to gather information. It is useful to cross-check your information by using two or more of these methods. Explain exactly how you conducted the evaluation.

12. Once the data are collected, arrange them in some order and use them to answer the questions you asked in the first place about the programme. Give a list of major findings and then a list of implications stemming from the findings. Finally give recommendations for the way forward.

13. Once the report is finished, plan ways of presenting it to the stakeholders, for example:
    - in one-to-one meetings with key people;
    - in general meetings of people such as participants;
    - in written or oral form.

If the report is not presented to all the stakeholders and decisions made on the way forward, it is not worth the trouble it took to write it.

Early Childhood Training Initiative evaluation plan

Area of operation ....

Organization ....

Names of participants

....

....

....

Preparation for the report (case study)

1. Factors affecting the work

(a) The learners

(b) **The context of the work**

Expected outcomes of the training	Ways to measure the quality of the results	Proposed evaluation activities

4. Presentation of highlights of plans

Objectives

To share highlights of each regional plan in order to enrich the learnings of each region and to build support for each regional team.

Materials needed

Flip-charts and pens.

Methods used

Group reports and plenary discussion.

Steps

1. The facilitator invites each group to briefly (five minutes each) present highlights of their plans to everyone.

2. As each group presents the highlights, the participants are given the opportunity to comment and to ask questions for clarity. The emphasis is on respectful, supportive reflections on the plans.

3. The participants and facilitators share their views on the patterns and programme issues they have heard in the range of presentations: for example, similarities in the plans, divergent or innovative strategies, etc.

4. The facilitators give their own plan of action for supporting the participants in the future.

5. Representatives of support agencies respond by sharing the plans of their agencies to offer material and technical assistance to the efforts in each area or organization.

Watch point

It is useful to have copies of the plans made for the facilitators and the participants.

Purpose

> to help participants
>   - to review the expectations and objectives of the training event
>   - to reflect on the meaning of the learning experiences
>   - to evaluate the effectiveness of the training event
>   - to make the transition from the learning experience back into the work situation
>   - to reflect on the training cycles and policy-influencing activities they have undertaken since the first training and planning event they themselves undertook

Training sessions

(TIMINGS ARE APPROXIMATE)

A. Shared reflections

1. Introduction and response to plans of action

(30 MINS)

2. Review of expectations and objectives

(1 HR)

3. Evaluation and closing ceremony

(1 HR)

B. Reflections on action

1. The 'More and Better' River: charting the journey

(2 HRS)

2. Personal stories of change

(2 HRS)

3. Final reflections

(1 HR 30 MINS)

CHAPTER 9

Reflections

A. Shared reflections

1. Introduction and response to plans of action

Objective

To begin formative evaluation of the implementation phase of the Initiative by reflecting as a group on the proposed regional training plans.

Preparation needed

Facilitators ask for volunteers from among the participants to prepare and present a warming-up activity for the section.

Methods used

Plenary discussion.

Steps

1. The facilitator welcomes everyone to this last session of the training event and invites the participants to present a short warming-up activity.

2. Participants are asked to reflect again on the broad themes in the participants' plans of action and to volunteer thoughts on these, especially with regard to how they can support each other until the next gathering of the group.

3. The facilitator then asks participants to discuss together, in pairs, their first actions on returning to their own places of work. These actions are shared with the group.

Watch point

This session should be short and to the point, and also be guided by the participants on time use. They may have exhausted their thoughts on the plans of action in the previous section; on the other hand, they may have had some insights that they wish to share with the group.

2. Review of expectations and objectives

Objective

To review the expectations and objectives of the training event in the light of the learning outcomes.

Materials needed

- flip charts stating the objectives of the Initiative and training event;
- the expectations of the learning groups that they wrote on the first day of the training event.

Method used

Small groups.

Steps

1. The facilitator introduces the session and asks the participants to review:
   - as individuals the personal expectations that they set at the beginning of the training programme;
   - in area or organizational groups the objectives and expectations of their constituencies as they had written them on the first day of the training programme.

2. Each group presents a report to the plenary on those objectives and expectations met and unmet.

3. The plenary then decides on plans of action for the objectives and expectations that remain unmet.

Watch points

Make sure that all sets of charts on which expectations are written are kept safely throughout the programme for this activity.

Key learning points on reviewing expectations

1. The expectations that are generated at the beginning of any training event should be reviewed at the end in order to start planning for further steps to be taken.

2. Checking carefully throughout the training programme that training needs are being met builds trust between the participants and the facilitators.

3. When there are expectations that have not been met by the end of the training event, plans of action can be made to deal with these during the follow-up period of the training either by the facilitators or by the participants themselves alone or in partnership with one another.

3. Evaluation and closing ceremony

Objectives

To evaluate the effectiveness of the training event.

Materials needed

- an evaluation form for each person;
- a large mural made up of sheets of flip-chart paper, labelled with the name of the training event and put up on the wall or laid on the floor.

Preparation required

The participants need to decide before the final day how they wish to plan the closing ceremony for the programme. A task team could be elected to deal with this.

Methods used

Individual work and pairs for a plenary discussion.

Steps

1. The facilitator gives evaluation forms to the participants and asks them to fill them in (named or anonymous as they wish).

2. They are handed in for collation by the facilitators.

3. The participants discuss the event in pairs for about two minutes (highlights and 'lowlights') and share their comments in plenary.

4. The participants are then invited to draw or write anything they wish on the composite mural that symbolizes the training event's meaning for them.

5. The facilitators then hand over to the participants for the closing ceremony.

Watch points

1. It is very useful for the facilitators to give their own comments on the training event in this session in the same way as the participants.

2. The survey sheets should be collated as quickly as possible by the facilitators and the results shared with the participants at the earliest possible opportunity, perhaps in a follow-up communication after the event.

Individual summary evaluation form

Please fill the form in by yourself and hand in to the facilitators who will collate the responses.

You may sign the form or not, as you wish.

1. To what extent were you **informed** about the purposes of the workshop? Circle one number.

not at all									completely
1	2	3	4	5	6	7	8	9	10

2. To what extent did **each** of the following **influence** you to come to the training? Circle one number for each item.

		no influence			extremely influential	
(a)	general interest	1	2	3	4	5
(b)	need to do your job differently	1	2	3	4	5
(c)	required by organization to participate	1	2	3	4	5
(d)	to confirm that what you are already doing is OK	1	2	3	4	5
(e)	a chance to network with others	1	2	3	4	5
(f)	other (please specify) _____	1	2	3	4	5

3. To what extent do you think that this workshop will make a **difference** in the way you do your job?

no difference									substantial difference
1	2	3	4	5	6	7	8	9	10

4. Overall, how would you rate the **usefulness** of this workshop?

not useful								extremely useful	
1	2	3	4	5	6	7	8	9	10

5. Overall, how would you rate the following about this workshop? Circle one number for each item.

		extremely poor			excellent	
(a)	learning methods or processes	1	2	3	4	5
(b)	organization and flow of activities	1	2	3	4	5
(c)	cultural competence of the workshop content and process	1	2	3	4	5
(d)	cultural competence of trainers	1	2	3	4	5
(e)	other (please specify) _____	1	2	3	4	5

6. To what extent did the workshop provide the following? Circle one number per item.

		not enough	on target	too much		
(a)	practical examples	1	2	3	4	5
(b)	time for discussion	1	2	3	4	5
(c)	practice time	1	2	3	4	5
(d)	opportunity to consider what will help or stop you from applying your learning	1	2	3	4	5
(e)	help in planning for application of learning	1	2	3	4	5
(f)	other (please specify) _____	1	2	3	4	5

7. To what extent would you describe your experiences in the workshop as follows? Circle one number for each item.

		not at all			completely	
(a)	relevant to your job	1	2	3	4	5
(b)	possible to apply	1	2	3	4	5
(c)	better than what you were doing	1	2	3	4	5
(d)	met your needs	1	2	3	4	5
(e)	met the needs of your organization	1	2	3	4	5
(f)	other (please specify)	1	2	3	4	5
	_____					

8. Overall, to what extent did the workshop lead to the following? Circle one number for each item.

		not at all			substantially	
(a)	increased knowledge or skills	1	2	3	4	5
(b)	encouraged links with others for support	1	2	3	4	5
(c)	changed attitudes or feelings	1	2	3	4	5
(d)	confirmed what you are already doing is OK	1	2	3	4	5
(e)	offered insights into doing your job differently	1	2	3	4	5
(f)	prepared you to apply learning	1	2	3	4	5
(g)	other (please specify)	1	2	3	4	5
	_____					

9. To what extent are you likely to do the following as a result of the workshop? Circle one number per item.

		not at all			extremely	
(a)	share information with others	1	2	3	4	5
(b)	make changes in how you do your work	1	2	3	4	5
(c)	use materials from the workshop	1	2	3	4	5
(d)	contact others for support to apply learning	1	2	3	4	5
(e)	actively encourage your organization to apply ideas from the workshop	1	2	3	4	5
(f)	get more training or information on topic	1	2	3	4	5
(g)	other (please specify)	1	2	3	4	5

_____

10. To what extent do you expect this workshop will make a difference in the way you do your job?

no difference								substantial difference	
1	2	3	4	5	6	7	8	9	10

11. To what extent do you feel able to apply your learning from this workshop to your job? Circle one number.

not at all								completely	
1	2	3	4	5	6	7	8	9	10

12. To what extent do the following exist in your organization or community to help you apply your learning? Circle one number for each item.

		not at all				substantially
(a)	sufficient resources	1	2	3	4	5
(b)	encouragement from others	1	2	3	4	5
(c)	opportunity to apply learning	1	2	3	4	5
(d)	authority to act or apply learning	1	2	3	4	5
(e)	support for making changes suggested in this workshop	1	2	3	4	5
(f)	other (please specify) _____	1	2	3	4	5

Please add any additional comments or suggestions you have about the workshop or your experiences.

Thank you.

B. Reflections on action

1. The 'More and Better River': charting the journey

Objective

To begin the process of identifying our progress (strengths and challenges) in each country within the last year.

Materials needed

- flip-charts and pens for each area or organizational group;
- one large diagram of the main River of the Initiative prepared by the facilitators identifying the sources of the Initiative and major events.

Methods used

- groups;
- drawing a symbolic 'map';
- plenary presentation.

Steps

1. The facilitator states the objective of the session, that this is a debriefing process at the beginning of this second training event.

2. The facilitator explains the concept of the whole Initiative as a river flowing through a continent.
   - Water is a symbol of life.
   - Starting in small high catchment areas, the water collects into streams and flows together into the wider waters of a river, eventually joining with other tributaries to form a large steadily moving river constantly moving towards the sea whence the water circulates the globe through the oceans.
   - There are times of drought and flood for the rivers.

   We have embarked upon this 'More and Better River' in many different types of craft, navigating rapids, broads and narrows, and stagnant pools, through dangers such as crocodiles and hippopotamuses. Through heroic acts, we have managed to harness resources such as fish, the flow of the river, rain and calm islands on which fruit grows.

We need to record our journeys in the Initiative (the river), and in its parts (tributary rivers and streams), so we can build up a composite allegory of the Initiative.

3. The facilitator then gives the task: in area or organizational groups:

    - draw your own regional Initiative tributary river;

    - draw and name the challenges and hindrances (and heroic acts you may have had to undertake) that have marked this last year since the previous training event we all attended.

4. Pin the 'tributary' to the board so that all tributaries drain into the main river, illustrated by the facilitators themselves as the experience of the Initiative as a whole.

5. Each regional team gives an explanation, or guided tour, of their 'tributary' and the facilitators guide them through the main river.

6. The participants are asked to synthesize the key learnings from this activity. Issues and themes that need further explanation are noted on a flip chart.

7. During the report back, each person makes a record of helpful ideas and challenges to themselves or to the Initiative in training and in policy. These are retained for synthesis in a later activity.

Watch points

Allow participants enough time to describe their 'journeys' down their rivers. Much rich information will come from this session: it is advisable to keep a flip chart handy for writing down key themes and issues as they emerge.

Key learning points

1. It is very important for all participants to be given a chance to report back as fully as possible on the experiences they have had during the implementation phases of a project.

2. This reporting-back process can be done by giving feedback that harnesses participants' creative (story-telling, drawing and symbolizing) capabilities.

3. Using such activities not only enables participants to synthesize key learning points for themselves and the group in a way that is interesting and to the point, but also avoids long and often boring descriptive reports of processes and products.

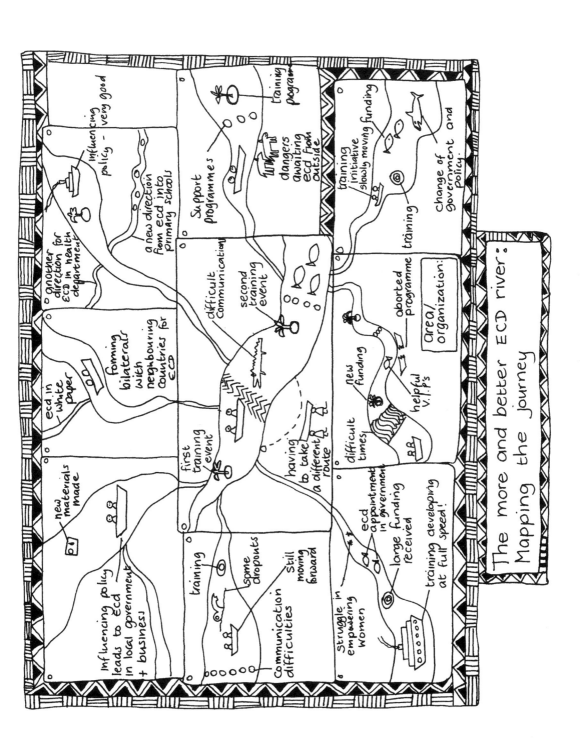

The more and better ECD river: Mapping the journey

Comments and ideas

Influencing policy	
Helpful ideas	**Problems/challenges**

Training programmes	
Helpful ideas	**Problems/challenges**

2.   Personal stories of change

Objective

To build confidence by sharing and confirming experiences of personal and professional development over the past period.

Preparation needed

If possible, a quiet venue where people can feel relaxed and thoughtful.

Methods used

Individual stories told in plenary.

Steps

1. The facilitator asks the participants to think of a story about the experiences of the past year since the previous training event and says: 'This will provide all of us with rich narrative lessons from which we can learn. Let us now narrate stories of professional and personal development we have experienced during the year. Listen for lessons.'

2. One by one, individuals tell short stories and others listen, and the facilitator encourages affirmation by the group.

3. The facilitator asks, 'What was it like to tell and hear these stories? What did we learn? How does this kind of story-telling affect our relations with each other in our group?'

Watch points

1. This activity requires a relatively intimate level of sharing, for which group members must be prepared. This is a good exercise with ongoing groups who know each other well.

2. It is possible to pre-select a participant who is willing to go first in order to break the ice and demonstrate the length and focus of presentation.

3.   Final reflections

Objectives

To reflect as a group on the key learnings of the training event.

Materials needed

A group reflection form for each group.

Methods used

Small groups.

Steps

1. The facilitator asks all participants to form small groups of five at most to reflect participatively on the training event.

2. Each group is given the Focus Group Reflection form for discussion.

3. A scribe in each group is asked to read through one question at a time, writing down the answers of the group members on the sheets provided.

4. The forms are given to the facilitators for collating.

5. The groups are then asked to make a general statement on the highlights and lowlights of the training event and to share these with the plenary.

Watch points

The participants need to be very sure of the instructions for the evaluation task. The Focus Group Reflection form may take a long time to complete. Encourage participants to continue to give full answers to each and every question.

Key learning points

1. Participative evaluation done through focus groups is a very relevant and rich way of conducting an evaluation.

2. A focus group is a small discussion group formed specifically to focus on an issue and to bring forward ideas for further discussion.

3. The facilitator reads through all the forms and collates all the points on to a master copy. The results of the focus group reflections are then given back to the participants for discussion as they wish.

Focus group reflection on the workshop

Question 1

Overall, what single word would you use to describe the programme and the areas it covered?

What was one of its most noticeable features?

Ask the group first for a one-word response to the workshop. Encourage discussion.

Other ways of drawing responses:

'Any reactions? Are any of you surprised at the words others came up with?'

Single words

Other specific features

Other comments

Question 2

'In general, what do you feel the primary objectives of the workshop were and do you think that these objectives were achieved?'

Other ways of asking the question:

'What do you think that the organizers of the training programme were trying to communicate to participants? Were they successful? Were the objectives achieved for you personally? How about for the group?'

Words and phrases used to describe objectives

Successful? In what ways? How many 'Yesses' and how many 'Noes'?

Reasons/other comments

Question 3

'As you think back over the various activities in the workshop, what type of participant do you think it was ideally designed for?'

Other questions to ask:

'Do you think that the organizers of the workshop had a particular type of participant in mind (for example, in terms of experience, training, knowledge, attitudes, etc.) Do you think that the focus should be revised? Why?'

Descriptions of the target participant

Suggested changes

Other comments

Question 4

'As you think back over the workshop, were there segments or components that you felt were more effective or that you liked more? Were there any that you felt were less effective?'

Other questions to ask:

'Would you suggest revising any part of the workshop in such a way as to make it more relevant and meaningful to the participants? Were any of the activities too complicated? Were any too simple?'

Most effective features of the workshop

Suggested changes and why

Other comments

Question 5

'As you think back over the workshop, are there any areas in which you needed more background or preparation prior to the training?'

Other questions to ask:

'Do you feel that any additional background materials could be integrated into the training? How?'

Areas in which more background was needed and why

Suggested changes/methods of integration

Other comments

Question 6

'When you finished the workshop, did you feel prepared to implement the plans of action developed in the training? To what extent? Did you feel more prepared with respect to some plans than others?'

Other questions to ask:

'Are there any areas in which you feel unprepared? Would you suggest revising the workshop in any way to increase participants' sense of being prepared? How?'

Perceptions of being prepared/not being prepared. Why?

Suggestions for improving perceived self-preparedness

Other comments

Question 7

'Were the training materials used as part of the training programme effective? Would you suggest changing them in any way? How?'

Other questions to ask:

'For example, are the materials clearly designed and easy to understand? Were they too long or did they focus too much on standard written text as compared with visual presentations (that is, pictures and charts)?'

Materials designed well/No change needed and why

Changes in materials suggested and why

Other comments

Question 8

'What about the facilitators who conducted the workshop – in what ways were they effective or ineffective? Why?'

Other questions to ask:

'Are there alternative facilitation styles or facilitator types that you would recommend?'

Ways that facilitators and facilitator styles were effective

Suggestions for changes in facilitators and facilitation styles

Other comments

Question 9

'Was there anything about the setting in which the workshop was conducted that contributed or detracted from the overall programme?'

Other questions to ask:

'For example, was the room quiet enough? Were there distractions or interruptions? Did anything about the setting make it difficult to concentrate?'

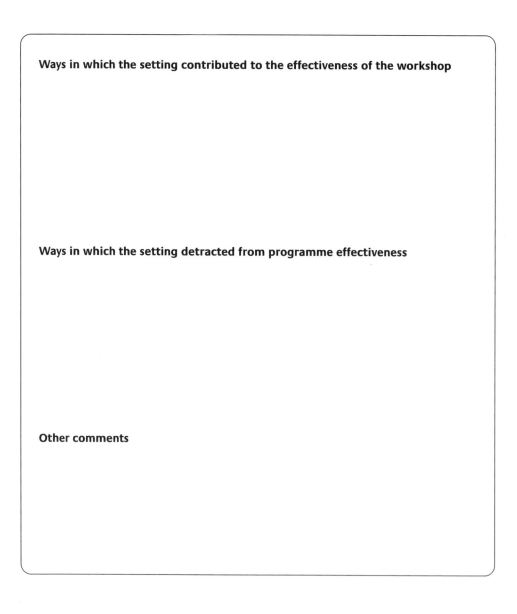

Ways in which the setting contributed to the effectiveness of the workshop

Ways in which the setting detracted from programme effectiveness

Other comments

Question 10

'Overall, did participating in the programme make you enthusiastic about carrying out the activities covered in the training? Are you motivated to tell others about these activities? Are you motivated to promote participation in the workshop to colleagues?'

Other questions to ask:

'If you are not enthusiastic, what changes in the programme might have increased your enthusiasm?'

YES, enthusiastic. Why?

NO, not enthusiastic. Why?

Other comments

CHAPTER 10

Tools for planning and evaluation

1. Methods used during the training event

This grid can be used as a guideline when planning sessions and activities for choosing appropriate methods for achieving objectives. It can also be used as a checklist for reflecting on the training event and the ways in which learning was planned and achieved.

Method	
Small-group discussion of about five individuals so that everyone has the opportunity to talk	
Plenary discussion plenary means full – the full group	
Working in pairs	
Individual work	
Brainstorming encouraging participants to give a list of responses quickly and widely before detailed discussion takes place	
Role play or drama	
Demonstration	
Ranking activity	
Community map	

Four Open Questions	
Case study	
Videotape/pictures	
Lectures and top-ups, summaries	
Using objects	
Nominal round report back each participant or group gives one point at a time round the group, until all points are given (this ensures that everyone gets a turn to speak)	
Diagrams and pictures as a way of reporting back to plenary	
Stories as a way of reporting to plenary	
Songs/poems as a way of reporting to plenary	
Gallery walk as a way of reporting back: all groups put their responses up on the wall for the plenary to read and discuss while walking around	
Categorizing by voting as a way of summing up the main points	
Short sessions	
Longer sessions	
Seated sessions	
Sessions where participants move about	

2. Follow-up questionnaire for participants

This questionnaire can be used to measure the views of participants on the training event once they are back in their places of operation and busy with their own training programmes.

1. What changes have you made in your training methods as a result of the training event?

2. What changes have you made in your role as a change agent as a result of the training event?

3. Overall, how would you rate the usefulness of the training event?

not useful								extremely useful	
1	2	3	4	5	6	7	8	9	10

4. To what extent would you describe your experiences in the training event as follows? Circle one number for each item.

		not at all				completely
(a)	relevant to your job	1	2	3	4	5
(b)	possible to apply	1	2	3	4	5
(c)	better than what you were doing	1	2	3	4	5
(d)	met your needs	1	2	3	4	5
(e)	met the needs of your organization/ community	1	2	3	4	5
(f)	other (please specify) _____	1	2	3	4	5

5. Overall, to what extent did the training event lead to the following? Circle one number for each item:

		not at all				completely
(a)	increased knowledge of key early childhood development areas	1	2	3	4	5
(b)	increased training knowledge or skills	1	2	3	4	5
(c)	encouraged links with others for support	1	2	3	4	5
(d)	changed attitudes or feelings	1	2	3	4	5
(e)	confirmed that what you were already doing was OK	1	2	3	4	5
(f)	offered insight into different training methods	1	2	3	4	5

		not at all			completely	
(g)	prepared you to apply experiential participatory learning methods	1	2	3	4	5
(h)	offered insights into different ways to influence policy	1	2	3	4	5
(i)	prepared you to act as an agent of change to influence policy	1	2	3	4	5
(j)	other (please specify) _____	1	2	3	4	5

6. To what extent did you do the following as a result of the workshop? Circle one number for each item.

		not at all			completely	
(a)	shared information with others	1	2	3	4	5
(b)	made changes in how you do your work	1	2	3	4	5
(c)	used materials from the training event	1	2	3	4	5
(d)	contacted others for support to apply learning	1	2	3	4	5
(e)	actively encouraged your organization to apply ideas from the training event	1	2	3	4	5
(f)	got more training and information on the topic	1	2	3	4	5
(g)	increased the number of experiential training activities	1	2	3	4	5
(h)	increased your efforts to influence policy	1	2	3	4	5
(i)	other (please specify) _____	1	2	3	4	5

7. To what extent did the workshop make a difference in the way you train?

no difference									substantial difference
1	2	3	4	5	6	7	8	9	10

8. To what extent do the following exist in your organization or community to help you to apply your learning? Circle one number for each item.

		not at all			sufficient	
(a)	sufficient resources	1	2	3	4	5
(b)	encouragement from others	1	2	3	4	5
(c)	opportunity to apply learning	1	2	3	4	5
(d)	authority to act or apply learning	1	2	3	4	5
(e)	support for making changes suggested during the training event	1	2	3	4	5
(f)	other (please specify)	1	2	3	4	5

_____

9. To what extent do you feel able to apply your learning from the training event to your current training activities? Circle one number.

not at all									completely
1	2	3	4	5	6	7	8	9	10

10. Please circle one number for each item that most closely reflects your opinion.

		strongly disagree				strongly agree
(a)	my training needs are well understood and accepted by my institution	1	2	3	4	5
(b)	I feel committed to acquiring the knowledge and skills needed to apply participatory training methods	1	2	3	4	5
(c)	I have the information and skills I need to influence training methods in my institution	1	2	3	4	5
(d)	I have a clear understanding of my role in bringing back to my institution and community the information and skills about participatory training methods	1	2	3	4	5
(e)	I am capable of transferring information back to my institution and community	1	2	3	4	5
(f)	I know what my learning needs are	1	2	3	4	5

11. Briefly describe the experiential participatory training plans and activities that you have carried out since the training event.

12. Describe the factors that have made it difficult for you to carry out these plans and activities. Refer to your own learning skills, your work, your environment.

13. Briefly describe the steps you have taken since the training event to influence early childhood development policy.

14. Describe the factors that have made it difficult for you to act as a change agent in order to influence early childhood policy. Refer to elements in the training event, you as the change agent, your environment.

15. Please add any additional comment or suggestions you have about the training event or your experiences.

This form has been adapted from the work of Judith Ottoson, Assistant Professor, Adult Education Research Center, The University of British Columbia, Vancouver, B.C., Canada, V6T 124.

3. Guidelines for facilitators when carrying out support visits to participants

Here are some possible questions that can be asked by facilitators of the participants when they are visiting them in order to give support.

Some questions are relevant when the visit coincides with a training event, while others can be asked at any time.

It is useful to go through the plans of action that the participants developed at the training event before visiting the participant.

1. Training events
   - What particular successes and challenges have you experienced in implementing the plans you developed for training?
   - How long did it take you to prepare for this training event and how did you prepare?
   - How did the participants on the training event that you facilitated respond to the participatory experiential approach? (Examples and quotations would be useful here.)
   - What modifications have you made to the activities in the training manual either to make them more culturally relevant or for other reasons, for instance time constraints?
   - If you ran a training event for a shorter time than the one you attended yourself, which activities did you leave out and why?
   - What new learning activities have you developed?
   - Have you translated any of the materials into your own language?
   - What methods did you use to form small learning groups during the training event?
   - When you started to plan the training event, how confident did you feel about taking on this task? What areas of doubt did you have and how did you overcome them?
   - Now that you have begun to train trainers, have you identified any important content or method areas that were missing or insufficiently covered in the training you attended? (Please give details.)
   - How much have you been able to use the participatory experiential method in your everyday work?
   - How were the participants whom you are training selected? Are some from non-governmental organizations as well as from government departments?

- Will you be able to follow up on the training you are giving through support visits to participants? What may help or hinder you?

- What sort of support have you managed to gain for the training and the method?

- What plans have been made to reach the parents and early childhood workers with this training?

2. Influencing policy

- What particular successes and challenges have you experienced in implementing the plan of action for influencing policy?

- What opportunities have you had to influence policy and raise awareness outside the plan of action you developed?

- How confident did you feel about carrying out this task?

- How have people responded so far to your activities?

- Who is supporting you in your efforts to influence policy?

- What new insights have you gained from the experiences you have had so far?

3. The participants on the training event

- Have you had any previous experience of the experiential participatory methods used in the training? How do these methods differ from those used in previous training courses?

- Which activities did you learn most from?

- What were your expectations when you came on the course and how did the reality fit in with your expectations?

- What have you learned from the way in which the facilitators worked together?

- How will you use this training to work with early childhood workers, and families and children?

- Which content and methods do you feel most comfortable using and why?

- Has the training changed you as a person? How?

- Whom do you train? Is it possible or desirable to include workers from other sectors, for instance health, welfare or education? How would you go about doing this?

4. Guidelines for writing reports

This guide for writing reports on progress of the training Initiative in each region was developed by the facilitators of the training Initiative with the participants.

The report will be most useful if it contains analysis as well as description, that is, comment on what is going well and why, and what is not going well and why not. Possible headings for the report are listed below.

1. Introduction

   Put the training event in the context of the whole training Initiative. Which event it is and what type of event, for example a follow-up course. There may need to be a brief description of the earlier course and progress to this latest point.

2. Planning for the training
   - Describe the process you undertook to recruit the participants and any problems you may have encountered in this.
   - Briefly describe the logistics, for instance the venue and distances to the venue.

3. The participants
   - How many participants are there on the course?
   - Have any of them had prior training?
   - What gender and age are they?
   - From what part of the country do they come?
   - In which sectors do they work?
   - What particular problems do they encounter in their daily work?

4. The training programme

   (a) The content
   - Organizing the content: how long was the training event and how was each day and week arranged in terms of sessions and breaks?
   - Did you follow the manual carefully? How did you adapt it?
   - Which content areas did you feel you covered well and which did you feel the participants particularly responded to?
   - Were there any content areas that you felt that you did not deal with adequately? Why do you think this happened?

- How did the participants evaluate the event? (Attach a copy of the questionnaire you used if it is different from those in the manual, as well as the responses you received.)

(b) The methods
- What was the participants' experience of participatory learning methods before attending this course?
- What were their responses to this method and how did you handle them?
- How did you as a facilitator respond to using this method with the participants?
- What new methods and activities did you introduce? (Attach copies of these.)

5. Plans for follow-up activities
- What are the main themes in the plans of action made by the participants?
- What arrangements have you made to give follow-up support to the participants?
- What will be the main areas of concern to you in these visits?

6. Conclusions
- What are your general feelings about the training course and progress?
- Are there any problems or challenges that have not been mentioned so far?
- What learning points need to be made for future training events?
- How did you find the experience of working as a co-facilitator in a team?

5. Self-evaluation instrument for trainers

This self-evaluation and monitoring tool for early childhood trainers was developed by the participants in the Early Childhood Joint Training Initiative. It can be used both as a self-evaluation checklist and as a peer-group discussion document.

A. PRE-PLANNING

	Self/team check
1. Learning about participants	
1.1 Identity, background and number of participants are ascertained as early as possible.	
1.2 Learning needs, interests, knowledge and any special logistical needs of the participants are identified as soon as possible.	
2. Preparing logistics	
2.1 Logistics, e.g. food, transport, venue, accommodation have been carefully planned.	
2.2 Adequate funding has been secured.	
2.3 A clear financial plan and bookkeeping system have been set up.	

B. DESIGNING TRAINING ACTIVITIES

3. Background preparation	
3.1 Content areas are thoroughly reviewed and researched.	
3.2 Key learning points for the event and for each session are formulated.	
3.3 Appropriate resource people and sources of technical information are identified.	

	Self/team check
4. Session planning	
4.1 Overall training themes and objectives are identified based on the criteria of relevance, appropriateness and feasibility.	
4.2 Written session plans are developed for each training session covering the following items: • theme • title • time • objectives/purpose • learning aids/materials • activities/steps • key learning points/messages • evaluation plan	
4.3 Objectives are clear, measurable and attainable.	
4.4 Key learning points or messages are highlighted.	
4.5 Learning aids/materials prepared are culturally appropriate and technically accurate.	
4.6 Methods selected are appropriate and effective: • built from the learners' experiences • successfully express and complement the content • logically sequenced/well placed • harmonized with the learning style of the participants.	
4.7 Participatory evaluation methods are planned.	

C. FACILITATING TRAINING SESSIONS

5. Knowledge	
5.1 Facilitator draws out from, starts with and values the experiential knowledge of the participants.	
5.2 Facilitator has a strong grasp of the content knowledge relevant to the session.	
5.3 Facilitator adds additional content/key learning points to fill key gaps in an appropriate, suitable way.	

	Self/team check
6. Skills	
6.1 Facilitator establishes a comfortable learning environment through an interesting variety of introduction, expectation and warming-up activities.	
6.2 Facilitator leads and manages a wide variety of active learning activities skilfully: • sets up and explains each activity clearly • helps participants and groups to clarify tasks • manages time effectively • orchestrates (co-ordinates) participation sensitively (with understanding of each participant's needs) • listens actively and carefully • acknowledges and synthesizes participants' knowledge • helps participants generate and summarize key learning points	
6.3 Facilitator is familiar with a wide variety of participatory experiential learning methods, such as: • brainstorming • group work • role plays • drama • fishbowl • demonstration • case-studies • discussion and debate • sequential questioning	
7. Interpersonal behaviour (stemming from the attitudes held by the facilitator)	
7.1 Facilitator shows empathy and understanding.	
7.2 Facilitator builds on the strengths of the participants.	
7.3 Facilitator accepts and respects differences.	
7.4 Facilitator shows friendliness and a sense of humour.	
7.5 Facilitator demonstrates flexibility.	
7.6 Facilitator remains actively engaged in all activities.	
7.7 Facilitator uses body language to communicate effectively.	
7.8 Facilitator gives and receives feedback effectively.	

D. REVIEWING AND EVALUATING TRAINING:

	Self/team check
8. Evaluation	
8.1 Evaluation is seen as an ongoing activity.	
8.2 Co-trainers and participants are invited to participate in evaluation.	
8.3 Feedback is built into the overall design and adjustments are made to the sessions and programme as necessary.	
8.4 Different techniques are used to accomplish various evaluation tasks, for example: • focus groups • questionnaires • verbal feedback • pictures • question-and-answer sessions • observation • review of records	
8.5 Facilitator maintains an open attitude towards evaluation feedback by: • accepting criticisms • respecting different viewpoints • models (displays) openness to feedback	

6. Guidelines for developing materials

Time

One day or more depending on time available.

Objectives

To develop materials relevant to the users' needs.

Materials needed

Flip-chart paper, pictures.

Methods used

Group work.

Steps:

1. The facilitator welcomes the participants at this workshop and conducts an activity on introductions: each person gives his or her name, home, occupation and tells everyone about his/her interest in children and in early childhood development.

2. The facilitator then asks participants to group themselves according to the area they come from (in groups of about five at most).

3. Each group then discusses the questions in the following tables and gives responses to the plenary group.

4. The plenary group finds points of commonality among the reports.

5. The facilitator then asks the groups to discuss what types of materials would be most useful for parent-support programmes.

6. A list of materials is generated by the groups.

7. Each group takes one category of material and brainstorms ideas for content and presentation.

8. These ideas are then presented to the plenary and task groups are set up to develop further the ideas using whatever technical support is necessary.

9. The groups then develop sets of questions and activities for use with the materials.

10. The facilitator then asks:
   - Who could use these materials?
   - What training and support are needed to assist them to use these materials?
   - How could the support be organized?

11. Plans of action for future development are made.

THE ENVIRONMENT OF THE CHILD

(a) How do families make a living (in general) in your area?

(b) Where do they live and in what type of shelter?

(c) Who generally makes up the family within the household?

(d) What is the role of the mother, father and other adults in the family? What do each of them do during the day?

THE CARE AND EDUCATION OF THE CHILDREN

(a) How do families look after their babies and children?

(b) Who looks after the children? What do the children do during the day?

(c) What do you think the health, nutrition and educational needs of the children are?

AREAS OF SUPPORT FOR PARENTS AND FAMILIES

(a) What do you think the main needs of parents and families are with regard to child care and education?

(b) How can parents best be contacted in your area and what would be the best approach to take when offering parent-support programmes within the community?

7. Useful reading

BERNARD VAN LEER FOUNDATION. Why Children Matter. Investing in Early Childhood Care and Development. The Hague, Bernard van Leer Foundation, 1994.

——. Building on People's Strengths: Early Childhood in Africa. The Hague, Bernard van Leer Foundation, 1994.

COVEY, S. R. The Seven Habits of Highly Effective People. Powerful Lessons in Personal Change. New York, Simon & Schuster, 1989.

DEVELOPMENT EDUCATION CENTRE. Us and the Kids: Ideas and Resources for Parent Groups. Birmingham, Development Education Centre, 1991.

FUGELSANG, A. Child Advocacy in Community Development. Sri Lanka, Redd Barna, 1989.

FUGELSANG, A.; CHANDLER, D. Basket of Ideas for Trainers. Norway, Redd Barna, 1994.

HOPE, A.; TIMMEL, S. Training for Transformation: A Handbook for Community Workers. Rev. ed. Zimbabwe, Mambo Press, 1984.

LANDERS, C. Off to a Good Start; A Time of Adventure: From One to Three Years; Pathways to Learning; Ready for School. New York, UNICEF, 1996. (Videos and facilitators' resource guides.)

TORKINGTON, K. The Rationale for Experiential/Participatory Learning. The Hague, Bernard van Leer Foundation, 1996.

TORKINGTON, K.; LANDERS, C. Enhancing the Skills of Early Childhood Trainers. The Hague/Paris, Bernard van Leer Foundation/UNESCO, 1995.

UNICEF. Early Childhood and Development. The Challenge and the Opportunity. New York, UNICEF, 1993.

VAN DER EYCKEN, W. Introducing Evaluation. The Hague, Bernard van Leer Foundation, 1992.

VELLA, J. Learning to Teach: Training of Trainers for Community Development. Save the Children/OEF International, 1989.